HEAD-AND-NECK CANCER KILLS…

"FIGHT'S ON!!!"

by

DON SUBLETT

ISBN 978-1-64079-315-6 (Paperback)
ISBN 978-1-64079-316-3 (Digital)

Christian Faith Publishing, Inc.
296 Chestnut Street
Meadville, PA 16335
www.christianfaithpublishing.com

Printed in the United States of America

DEDICATION

This book is dedicated to Dr. Andrea McMurphy.
Your calm and confident demeanor, and aggressive
"take no prisoners" approach established my attitude
for beating this cancer!
Dr. Mac, you exemplify all that a person could
want or hope for in their physician. Simply,
you are the best!

CONTENTS

"Then Jesus told his disciples a parable to show them that they should always pray and not give up."
Luke 18:1 (NIV)

INTRODUCTION

Some of the most difficult words a person will most likely ever hear are, "There is concern for _____." You fill in the blank. It could be stroke, heart attack, Leukemia, or any of a multitude of life-threatening diseases. In my case, those words were "cancer at the base of the tongue." This was the tentative diagnosis I was given on March 22 by one of the general surgeons at the Eglin Air Force Base Regional Hospital in Fort Walton Beach, Florida.

Immediately after the tentative diagnosis, the doctor told me he would not be the one treating me and I was referred to the hospital's Ear, Nose, and Throat (ENT) Clinic. Dr. (Maj.) Andrea McMurphy—Dr. Mac—then became my doctor. During a tongue biopsy three days later, on March 24th, she confirmed there was, in fact, squamous cell carcinoma in the base of the tongue. Prior to being diagnosed, I didn't know there was such a thing as tongue cancer. Suddenly, I was becoming fully immersed in the treatment of it.

What causes base-of-tongue cancer, and who is likely to get it? The exact cause of base-of-tongue cancer is unknown. However, the National Cancer Institute, or NCI, website[1] lists the following as possible causes: smoking and chewing tobacco; heavy alcohol use; a diet low in fruits and vegetables; drinking maté, a stimulant drink common in South America; chewing betel quid, a stimulant commonly used in parts of Asia; and being infected with human papillomavirus (HPV).

I smoked for about fifteen years when I was much younger, but it had been over thirty years since I smoked my last cigarette. It was equally as long since I was a moderate drinker and I never chewed tobacco or used snuff. The remaining possible causes listed were non-factors, so, of the listed possibilities, smoking and drinking were the only possible causes which offered any explanation.

As incongruent as it may seem, the Veteran's Administration links Agent Orange exposure in South Vietnam as a possible cause of esophageal and laryngeal cancer, but not cancer in the base of the tongue. I did serve in Vietnam, so Agent Orange exposure could be a contributor. Regardless of the cause of the cancer, it was something that had to be dealt with. However, if possible, it would have been nice to know the cause.

Typically, the NCI website says, "…base-of-tongue cancer usually involves patients in the fifth through seventh decades of life; men are afflicted three to five times more often than women…" I was fifty-eight when diagnosed. NCI's website also says there are only about 2,500 cases of base-of-tongue cancer diagnosed in the United States each year, and about 123,000 worldwide. While not necessarily rare, base-of-tongue cancer is uncommon.

One question everyone diagnosed with cancer, especially a Stage 4 cancer, probably asks is, "Could the cancer have been discovered sooner?" I, too, asked myself the same question. The NCI website lists the following as possible symptoms for base-of-tongue cancer: a sore throat that does not go away; a dull pain behind the breastbone; a chronic cough; trouble swallowing; weight loss for no known reason; ear pain; a lump in the back of the mouth, throat, or neck; and a change in voice. Another source, which I cannot recall, listed a "hanging sensation" in the back of the throat as a possible sign.

A swollen lymph node proved to be definitive, but the only other possible indicator I experienced was the hanging sensation in the throat. There were only a couple of times I recalled experiencing this sensation and it didn't seem like cause for concern, because it went away after a day or two. Had I not discovered the swollen lymph node, I might not have realized for a very long time that there was something seriously amiss. In a word, I was "healthy."

Base-of-tongue cancer is classified as a "head-and-neck cancer" and I learned early on that treatment for any head-and-neck cancer is among the most—if not *the* most, outright—painful of any cancer treatment. This knowledge was extremely sobering. After the cancer diagnosis was confirmed, I began looking on the internet for information on base-of-tongue cancer and what I could expect as treatment unfolded. I wanted to know about other peoples' experiences with this particular cancer, but that type of information was almost impossible to find. Dr. Moore, the ENT clinic chief, recommended a couple of websites in addition to the NCI's, but they proved to be difficult to learn much from. There were questions and answers posted, but very little seemed pertinent to my concerns, nor could I find any chat sessions where information could be readily exchanged.

As noted above, there is considerable information of a general nature available on the NCI website. I found it helpful in an overall sense, but it still didn't provide me any insight into what to expect while undergoing treatment. Nor was there a local head-and-neck cancer support group, because of the small number of cases. (There would be a cancer support group formed later at the Eglin AFB Hospital, and as chance would have it, three-fourths of the initial attendees were head-and-neck cancer patients.) Even though the ENT doctors were very helpful in answering questions and explaining things, there were still answers they did not have.

A bit later, I was very fortunate to learn Walt Leirer, a fellow church member, was a five-year survivor of base-of-tongue cancer. I later came into contact with another individual in Mobile, AL, Sanford Flach, who recently completed treatments for the same cancer. Both Walt and Sanford proved to be valuable sources of information, and tremendous encouragers, as my treatments progressed.

Soon after learning I had base-of-tongue cancer, I sent an e-mail to let a small number of people know what was going on and to update them on my progress in getting treatment started. Our church secretary, Paula Willcox, took the liberty of forwarding my message to the church e-mail list, asking for prayers on behalf of my wife, Judy, and me. Once Paula forwarded a couple of my e-mails, I decided to take this task over so she wouldn't feel compelled to continue doing so.

So, I borrowed the church's e-mail list, began adding other friends to it, and continued to provide updates on my condition. Soon, I learned many people receiving the updates were forwarding them to other people and places around the world. In fact, it wasn't long before I began receiving messages from people I didn't know, asking to be included on future updates. I marveled at such kindness and concern from people I didn't know, and would likely never meet this side of heaven.

I have no solid idea of how many people ultimately received the updates, nor how many wound up praying for me. However, I do know I wound up with well over two hundred people on my "update" e-mail list, and I suspect there may have been a thousand or more individuals praying regularly, and often, for me. This estimate does not include the number of churches who added me to their prayer list, and the prayers offered during assemblies and Bible classes. I know there were many people routinely praying for me and I am grateful for each and every one.

When I began providing updates on my treatments and condition, I had no idea the updates would be received as warmly as they were, nor did I realize just how encouraging the responses to my e-mail updates would be to Judy and me. (I can now begin to barely understand how much the Apostle Paul might have been encouraged by the writings he received.) At about the mid-point of my treatments, I began receiving suggestions that my updates be incorporated into a book, once treatments were completed. I pooh-poohed that idea and never really gave it serious consideration. My motivation in sending out updates on my condition was twofold: (1) to force myself to confront what was going on and to think through the ramifications; and (2) to keep people involved in my cancer treatment and to continue to encourage them to pray for Judy and me.

Even after treatments were over and I continued to send out periodic updates, more people urged me to consider putting the updates into print, in order to tell my story. I remained hesitant to do so. However, friends persisted in their encouragement for me to reconsider. They evidently saw something I could not see in the updates, which would be beneficial and encouraging to future readers regarding the power of prayer, and reliance upon God to see us through the difficult times, especially when facing cancer.

The following e-mail was just one of several that finally convinced me to press ahead with this effort in hopes that telling my story would be encouraging to people facing cancer difficulties, and that it might be particularly beneficial to people with head-and-neck cancer.

-----Original Message-----
From: Linda Allen
Sent: Thursday, October 19, 10:24 PM
To: Don Sublett
Subject: Re: Finally!!!

Don... you are so amazing. I do wish you would consider writing a book... just an outline for people looking cancer in the face and taking it on WITH GOD'S HELP! Tell them about your updates, and even include them, and how much they helped you (and how much they helped us!). You are a wonderful writer.

I am so happy for you that you now have the feeding tube out. I continue to thank God for your outlook on it all, and for healing you. May God bless you as you come into contact with people who need your experiences to be related to them. Your life will touch so many... and I know God will always be praised if you or I am telling the story.

Much love to you & Judy.

Linda

After much encouragement and prayerful consideration, I chose to relate my experience in fighting cancer at the base-of-the-tongue, hoping it will be beneficial to you, or to someone you know who is (or will be) undergoing treatment for a head-and-neck cancer, or for that matter, any cancer or life threatening illness. I have absolute faith and belief that God is here to help, if we let Him into our lives.

I.

The Cancer Diagnosis

My cancer experience began when I awoke one morning around Christmas with a sore lymph node on the left side of my neck. I knew swollen lymph nodes were not normal, so I kept track of the swollen node for a few days. When the swelling didn't subside, I made an appointment to see my primary care doctor at the medical clinic on Hurlburt Field, FL. Figuring I had an infection of some sort, I expected to be given an antibiotic and then be sent on my way. However, the doctor's approach was to wait four to six weeks, since these things "tend to subside on their own." I accepted the doctor's diagnostic approach and left a few days later, in early January, for three weeks of work at Nellis Air Force Base (AFB), which is just north of Las Vegas, Nevada.

I retired from the United States Air Force, after more than twenty-nine years of service, and worked as a contractor for a company that helped plan and execute large-scale experiments for the Air Force. We did the bulk of the planning from our home station, at Hurlburt Field, FL., but the execution of the event usually occurred at Nellis AFB, Nevada, and other locations around the continental United States. We worked a two-year planning and execution cycle and were just beginning the execution phase of the experiment. Interestingly, each of these "wait and see" periods I was to work through conveniently fit around planned work events at Nellis AFB. During the time I worked at Nellis AFB, I continued to monitor the lymph node and noticed that the swelling was not subsiding. However, I didn't notice it getting any larger either… or, so I thought.

About a week after returning from Nevada, I made a follow-up appointment with my primary care doctor on Hurlburt Field. The doctor was not quite ready to give up on the node returning to normal on its own and suggested we wait two more weeks, which we did. During that two week period, I was given a new primary health care provider. (The military is always transferring people for one reason or another, so it is not uncommon at some point to find your primary care health manager has changed.)

My new doctor decided during my first appointment that it was time to use some diagnostic tools to figure out what was going on. So, she put in a request to Tri-Care (the military health care system) for an ultra-sound of the neck and also requested a referral to the Surgery Clinic on Eglin AFB across town, with the recommendation to the surgeon that I receive a CT scan. Within a week, I was notified of an appointment for the ultra-sound in Fort Walton Beach, as well as an appointment in the Surgery Clinic at Eglin AFB.

I went to the ultra-sound appointment and learned not only did I have a swollen lymph node on the left side of my neck, but I also had one of equal size on the right side! The diagnosis of the second swollen lymph node was a total surprise to me, since it was hidden behind structure. The tech's reaction was, "They are going to want to get those out of there." My reaction?

"I am *not* looking forward to this—particularly neck surgery—if that is what is in store for me."

Little did I realize at the time, but having to undergo neck surgery would have been mild compared to what I was about to experience.

A couple days after the ultra-sound was done, I went to my appointment with a surgeon on Eglin AFB. He concurred with my Hurlburt doctor's recommendation for a CT scan (with a seafood-based contrast dye) and sent me to Radiology to schedule the appointment. Radiology didn't have an appointment available for about three weeks. Due to the lengthy wait, I was told I could be referred "off-base" if I didn't want to wait that long for the scan. Once again, the three week wait fit conveniently around another scheduled work trip to Nellis AFB. So, I took the appointment for three weeks out, which was the day after my expected return from Nellis AFB. I am thankful I opted to take the appointment three weeks out, because it locked me into staying within the military healthcare system. After spending those twenty-nine years on active duty in the Air Force, I was both very comfortable with, and partial to being seen by, doctors "on-base." So, I went to Nellis AFB to work and returned to have the CT scan with contrast the next morning, after my return. The CT scan launched the most difficult challenge of my life.

I never planned to document my experience and treatment in this manner. It just seemed to happen. Looking back, I am very glad I did, because I benefited tremendously from the interaction with many people through the e-mail exchanges. What follows are the updates I sent to my group of faithful friends and prayer warriors, as well as some of the e-mails I received in return, along with my response to them. Had I realized at the time that the updates on my condition would be used as the basis for a book about my experience, I would have been more detailed in some areas when preparing them. Thus, my response to some of the e-mails I received now adds details which might have otherwise been excluded. Additionally, the responses I received to my updates will enable you to see in a very small way just how much I was encouraged by those supporting, and praying, for my wife and me. The reason I say "a very small way" is, I include just a small number of the total e-mail responses I received. Where appropriate, I will also provide additional comments.

-----Original Message-----[2]
From: Don Sublett
Sent: Friday, March 24, 5:42 PM
To: Support Group
Subject: Health Concern

Friends,

I was diagnosed earlier this week with cancer at the base of the tongue. Judy and I just returned from Eglin after having a biopsy of that area of the tongue and it confirmed the doctor's diagnosis. It is a Stage 4A cancer, but that is probably not as bad as it sounds, though it is certainly serious. This particular cancer usually doesn't present itself until it is at Stage 4. Mine graded at 4A, which is the lowest of the three Stage 4 cancer grades. That simply means it has spread beyond the tongue, but is not widely spread. The CT scan shows it in two lymph nodes in the neck, the tongue, and nowhere else. We can thank God for that!

Perhaps God's hand is already at work here. The reason I say that is, about three months ago, I woke up and the left side of my neck was sore. I felt the area and discovered a lymph node which was swollen. So, I went to the doctor and began the process which led to what we know today. That was the *only* time I have experienced any soreness in the lymph nodes. Had I ignored that sign, I could have easily found myself in worse condition than I am.

My doctor is encouraged because a lot of people with this condition don't begin pursuing treatment until after the cancer has really begun spreading. She considers me to be in "good shape, for the shape I am in." The doctor also says the cancer responds well to chemo and radiation, and I expect to begin a series of thirty-five (radiation) treatments soon.

Judy and I deeply appreciate the support and encouragement we have received from our friends, already, in the brief time we've been experiencing this. We covet your prayers and greatly appreciate your friendship, and love.

Don

Dr. McMurphy was very matter-of-fact, but also very encouraging to me during my initial visit with her. She also introduced me to Dr. Moore, the ENT Clinic Chief.

Dr. McMurphy explained how we would proceed in the treatment of the cancer—radiation and chemo first, with surgery as a last resort. She also emphasized the painful nature of the treatment and told me that having a strong support group would be very important and beneficial. Dr. McMurphy was optimistic due to the fact we had probably caught the cancer about as early as possible. Fortunately, I began pursuing a diagnosis immediately upon discovery of the swollen lymph node, whereas, many people choose to ignore the early signs and don't show up in the clinic until the lymph nodes are very large (four centimeters or larger) and distant metastasis is a major concern.

Shortly after Dr. McMurphy gave me the Stage 4 diagnosis, I called a very good friend, Ray Willcox, an elder in our congregation. I told Ray I had just been diagnosed with base-of-tongue cancer. (Ray had recently completed radiation treatments for prostate cancer, and was all too familiar with the emotions experienced from being diagnosed with cancer.) Ray and his wife, Paula, were out of town when I called, but he spread the word of my cancer among the church leadership. Word of my cancer then spread very quickly and our friends and church family rallied around us immediately. In fact, I had hardly gotten home when another of the elders, Mike Boucher, was ringing the doorbell. He spent a good deal of time helping me sort through some of the emotions I was feeling at the moment. My wife, Judy, teaches school and, though aware of the diagnosis, had not gotten home yet.

In retrospect, I treated being staged at 4A in somewhat of a nonchalant manner, because I knew absolutely nothing about cancer staging. Nor did anyone explain to me at the time just how serious it was.

I automatically assumed that, because the cancer did not have me on my knees, there was a Stage 5. I was pretty taken aback when I learned there is no Stage 5. Stage 4 is about as bad as it gets. However, by the time I learned the seriousness of being diagnosed at Stage 4, my mindset regarding fighting the cancer was already set. I was going to "beat" it.

Dr. McMurphy could have conveyed the news regarding the staging of my cancer in a cautionary and fatalistic manner, but she did not. Instead, Dr. McMurphy was upbeat, positive and encouraging in every way as she mapped out the plan for moving ahead.

My doctors all commented on my positive attitude throughout my treatment and felt that attitude was ultimately reflected in the outcome. I firmly believe that the doctor's attitude toward the patient is *also* reflected in the patient's attitude. Dr. McMurphy could not have been a better example for me to follow in that regard. She set the stage!

II.

Getting Ready To Begin Treatments

-----Original Message-----
From: Don Sublett
Sent: Tuesday, March 28, 6:02 PM
To: Support Group
Subject: Update

All,

This is my first shot at building a mass mailing list; but it really was not that difficult. So, I thought I would provide the status on where we stand now. Then, as things change, I will provide additional updates.

First, though, Judy and I really appreciate the overwhelming support and encouragement we have received from so many of you, already. The phone calls, cards, e-mails, visits, and most of all, the prayers really have our spirits up. We know we are not in this alone, and that is so uplifting.

We are still in the stage of getting everything lined up. Things continue to move pretty quickly and we are grateful for that. The sooner we get these next seven or eight weeks behind us, the better off we will be. I had a follow-up CT scan today, on the lungs, liver, chest, and abdomen. The doctor thinks everything is clean, but is not content to just "think" things through.

I also received appointments today with a nutritionist, as well as with a Radiation Oncologist with 21st Century Radiation Oncology in Fort Walton Beach, who will be administering the chemo. Both are for next Tuesday. Still to come are appointments with the dentist and the radiologist. I expect to have those set within the next couple of days. Judy and I will meet tomorrow with my ENT (Ear, Nose and Throat) doctor to follow up on last Friday's biopsy, and whatever else she might have in mind.

We will be glad when all of the blanks are filled in. We know the treatments are going to be difficult, but we have to view the chemo and radiation as our friends, and that is going to probably be pretty tough. Still, the chemo and radiation, along with your prayers and God's help, are going to kill the cancer.

That is about it for now. Again, we appreciate the support and covet your continued prayers.

Don

The first few days after the initial diagnosis and biopsy were pretty anxious ones. No matter how fast you are being moved through the system—and I know for a fact that I was moved very rapidly—it just doesn't seem like it is fast enough. It was good for me to step back and take a deep breath to help see just how quickly things were moving. In my case, Tri-Care seemingly acknowledged that days mattered when dealing with cancer in Stage 4. From diagnosis to the start of treatment was a month.

I learned the oncologists will not rush into a treatment regimen just for the sake of getting someone in treatment. The treatment schemes require considerable time and effort to plan. Administering the radiation to the head and neck is a very precise process, which factors in many variables. There are many clinical chemotherapy trials on-going and I know my chemotherapy oncologist did considerable research before settling on the combination of drugs I was administered.

-----Original Message-----
From: Don Sublett
Sent: Wednesday, March 29, 10:11 PM
To: Support Group
Subject: Another Update

Wow! What another interesting day Judy and I had. We spent, probably, ninety minutes this morning with my ENT doctor. Dr. McMurphy is our "quarterback."

Yesterday's CT scan showed clean in the liver, chest, and abdomen. There was one small (6mm) something, which showed in the lower left lung, but the radiologist seemed to think it was nothing. If it did prove to be significant, it would not alter the course of treatment I am scheduled for. I still have a one-inch tumor on the left side of the tongue, at its base, and it has moved into a lymph node on each side of the neck. This, we already knew, except for the tumor's size, but it was again confirmed.

Dr. Mac went over numerous items with us, and at my request, elaborated on the physiological changes I can expect during and after the treatment. Suffice it to say, all will not be as it once was, particularly in the mouth. I can expect to lose my saliva glands and taste buds. The taste buds will most likely return, but the saliva glands will be gone. This, along with radiated jaw bones, poses potentially significant dental problems. Saliva lubricates, but also assists in oral hygiene. Tooth extractions are almost impossible to heal and infections can much more easily go systemic.

Thus, it is important that I have a good oral evaluation prior to beginning treatment. To this end, she pursued getting me seen in the Eglin Dental Clinic, and was successful. I have an appointment on Monday and am confident; whatever dental problems might arise, we now have means to address them. Eglin has a dental residency program and it looks like I am one of their guinea pigs (and glad to be so!).

Dr. Mac was particularly interested in guiding us (going through Tri-Care) to a specific chemo oncologist. (I was confused yesterday when I said I had a chemo appointment set. It was for radiation.) Wheels were set in motion and I am confident the doctor will get what she wants.

Then, just in case things weren't going well enough, already, for us, she requested we have a "patient advocate" within Tri-Care. First time I ever heard of such a thing, but we now have one. This lady's role is to intervene on our behalf, in the event we feel we are being stonewalled or are not getting the treatment, or consideration, we think is warranted. It seems like God is opening doors before the walls are even erected.

Probably the most disconcerting thing about the visit was, I walked away thinking, it sounds like I will be getting radiation and chemo simultaneously. I suppose that might have been in the works from inception, but it obviously blew right by me—if that, in fact, is what will be happening. I will not know for certain what my treatment regimen will be until I actually see both oncologists and they coordinate what is best to treat my cancer. The one real benefit to combining the two, if warranted, and if I can tolerate them together, is that it is supposed to raise the survival probabilities by a few percentage points. That is certainly something for consideration, and lots of prayer.

This has been a remarkable eight days. It was only last Wednesday morning I was told, "There is concern for cancer." We have gone from concern, to confirmation, to being scheduled with a radiation oncologist, with more to come. We have also been touched in innumerable ways by your concern and prayers for our well-being, and healing. Judy and I ask you to continue to pray for us, and we also ask that you add Dr. McMurphy to your prayers. She will be flying to Chicago on Monday to take her board exams. We have every confidence she will do well on her boards, but know God can help ease her concerns, just as He is easing ours.

Don

****

All too often people tend to just breeze from one step to the next without stopping to say thanks along the way. Thus, I was compelled to write the Eglin AFB Hospital Commander a note, complimenting his people on the care provided during a very busy week for us.

Many people, both military and civilian, consider the military healthcare system to be substandard. Like many, I have heard stories about people being misdiagnosed and/or mistreated. No doubt, some of those stories have some merit to them, because no healthcare system is perfect. However, I have no doubt that today's military healthcare system is not my father's. The emphasis today is on quality health care and treatment, and at least in this area, it shows. I cannot say enough good things about the wonderful health care provided to us, and I most certainly can say nothing bad about that same care.

Of note is that the Eglin ENT Clinic was focused on the team approach, coordinating with all clinics necessary to help ensure the best possible outcome for its patients. In my case, the clinics engaged were Oncology, Nutrition, Dental and Patient Affairs. ENT doctors were also closely engaged with the Radiologists at 21st Century Radiation Oncology in Fort Walton Beach.

Below is my letter to the Eglin AFB Hospital Commander, as well as his response.

-----Original Message-----
From: Sublett Donald W.
Sent: Friday, March 31, 7:17 AM
To: Forthman, Gary S. Col. MIL USAF 96 MDG/CC
Subject: Thankful Appreciation

Colonel Forthman,

Sir, you must be absolutely bursting with pride at the privilege of being able to command an organization of so many fine people. FYI, I have had somewhat of a whirlwind experience this last couple of weeks, since being diagnosed with cancer at the base of the tongue. I think it is important for you to know that everywhere my wife, Judy, and I have turned, we have been met with the most professional, concerned, courteous, and most important, perhaps, personal attention to our needs imaginable. I know this will be somewhat lengthy as I share with you.

This experience began with a referral to the Eglin Surgery Clinic by my provider at Hurlburt Field. I was examined by Dr. P. K. and he ordered a CT of the neck, as was requested. TSgt Knoll performed the CT, and when I mentioned the area of concern was in a particular area, he said, "Here, let's tilt the neck so we might get a little better view." Was it that attention to detail which enabled the diagnosis?

A few days later, I went back to see "Dr. P.K.," as he is called by the staff. As easily as possible, he told me, "There is concern for cancer at the base of the tongue." After just a few seconds, that hit me like the proverbial ton-of-bricks and I had to lie back on the exam table to gather myself. Dr. P.K. had already told me that, unfortunately, he would not be able to continue my case, and that I would be referred to ENT. While I was trying to quiet the sound of the blood rushing through my ears, he went out, picked up the phone, and called ENT. Dr. P.K. came back in and told me to stop by ENT on my way out. As I walked into ENT, the receptionist was already booking me an appointment for 8:20 the next morning, with Dr. McMurphy.

On 23 March, I walked into Dr. McMurphy's exam room and she proceeded to give me her diagnosis. Dr. McMurphy also told me she had taken the liberty of scheduling me for a biopsy the next day. She said she didn't know how aggressively I wanted to pursue this, but that she could cancel if we were moving too quickly. I assured her that I felt faster was better! Of note regarding that visit is, Dr. McMurphy spent well over an hour examining me and discussing my cancer. I don't know if there were other patients behind me or not, but Dr. McMurphy's concern at that time was *me*. (I will try to remember that the next time I might sit in a waiting room past my appointment time.)

Since I was scheduled for the biopsy the next day, I had several stops to make—admissions/ anesthesiology, x-ray, and EKG. Everyone was so kind and considerate, even without knowing what my particular concern was. The next morning, my wife and I reported to the Ambulatory Surgical Unit (ASU) for the biopsy. What a remarkable group of professionals. Everyone was bent on easing anxieties and concerns, and certainly did so.

We followed up on the biopsy results this past Wednesday with Dr. McMurphy. No surprises, since she properly diagnosed what we are dealing with. Once again, Dr. McMurphy spent a huge amount of time with us going over treatment options and physical concerns, particularly dental. Dr. McMurphy had already requested a referral to the Eglin Dental Clinic. I realize that

I am retired and have no claim to any kind of dental care. Yet, I received a call from the Dental Clinic, Wednesday afternoon, with an appointment for Monday morning. If I am to be a guinea pig, then I am proud to serve!

One unusual wrinkle (I think) is Dr. McMurphy requested that I have a patient advocate, and Ms. Jane H. was present for the Wednesday appointment. Dr. McMurphy, Ms. H., my wife, and I all discussed my needs and appointments in detail. A chemo oncology appointment was lagging and Ms. H. immediately set out to get that established. Yesterday morning, I received a call from a Senior Airman in the Oncology office to tell me the Tri-Care computers were down, but that the Oncologist, Dr. Prieto, would be seeing me next week. How nice it was for her to call and tell me that.

One additional comment regarding Dr. McMurphy; she flies to Chicago on Monday for her medical boards. I know Dr. McMurphy must be under tremendous pressure due to that fact, alone. Yet, in our every dealing, she has given me her totally focused and undivided attention. I consider that remarkable, given the circumstances. We have every confidence in her success in passing the boards and are backing that with much prayer from a lot of folks.

If you share this e-mail, please don't remove the following. People really appreciate it when practiced leadership starts at the top. They also need to know that fact. In that vein, whether you recall or not, one morning, a week or so ago, I was showing my wife where the surgery clinic moved to. I knew where we were going, but we probably still looked a little bit confused. You were in the hallway and stopped us to ask if you could help. That "May I help you?" attitude is typical of *everyone* we have come in contact with in the Eglin Hospital. We saw, personally, that Eglin Hospital's "service attitude" obviously starts at the top and permeates to the lowest levels.

Finally, Judy and I accept that, ultimately, God is in control of my condition. Yet, we also acknowledge that God has put us in the midst of some of the finest helpers, technicians, and doctors in the United States Air Force, or anywhere. Even though retired, we are still very, very proud, and thankful, to be part of such a wonderful community of professionals.

Very Respectfully,

Donald W. Sublett, Maj. (R.), USAF

-----*Original Message*-----
From: Forthman, Gary S. Col. MIL USAF 96 MDG/CC
Sent: Monday, April 03, 1:46 PM
To: Sublett Donald W.
Subject: RE: Thankful Appreciation

Major Sublett,

Thank you for taking the time to send me this inspiring e-mail. It is certainly not only a testimony to the care you received while here at Eglin, but most importantly, to the gracious God we serve. Rest assured that I will pass this along to the right people for appropriate recognition. You and yours will certainly be in our prayers for a quick, complication-free recovery. Thanks for your service, both past, present, and future.

Warmest Regards,

Gary S. Forthman, Colonel, USAF
Commander

As I described to Colonel Forthman, I was literally floored by the diagnosis and had to lie back on the exam table shortly after Dr. P.K. gave me the news. Blood was coursing through my veins so loudly I could hardly hear the doctor as he spoke to me when he returned to the exam room. I had read about the blood pounding in the ears, but I had never experienced it. I can assure you from this experience that it actually does happen!

Receiving a cancer diagnosis is a stunning moment because, in the course of those few seconds, you realize you are, indeed, a mortal being. I previously knew, in what I can only describe as an academic sense, I would die one day. In an instant, that fact became very real. It was no longer academic. I internalized the fact that death is, indeed, real, though it wasn't necessarily imminent. It is a life-changing moment when the reality of your mortality is driven home so emphatically.

****

-----Original Message-----
From: Don Sublett
Sent: Wednesday, April 05, 4:47 PM
To: Support Group
Subject: RE: Another Update

Hi, Everyone!

It has been close to a week since my last update. Since that time, I have had several folks ask to be added to the mailing list and some have had e-mails forwarded to you. Those I am aware of are included here. I am grateful for your interest and concern. Everyone should feel free to send these notes to anyone and everyone you think might have an interest. Since the last update, I have been to the Dental Clinic on Eglin and have seen my Radiation Oncologist in Fort Walton Beach.

I must tell you, the folks at Eglin are a wonderful group of people. There is nothing lacking in our care—nothing whatsoever. Three doctors in the Dental Clinic spent over an hour with me on Monday morning, discussing how to maintain my present dental health and the anticipated effects from the radiation. No real surprises in what they told me. Basically, we don't ever want to have to pull a tooth, because the healing process in the lower jaw will be severely impacted. They have also made me "trays" which I am to use for daily fluoride treatments. The prosthodontist told me to come back in July or August and he would make me any new dental appliances needed. I am so fortunate.

Today, Judy and I met with Dr. Bonanno, my Radiation Oncologist. Dr. Bonanno didn't tell us a whole lot we did not already know, or suspect. However, he did say there will be more than 35 radiation treatments, but didn't say how many more. That may not be known until I actually begin treatment, which should be sometime about ten days out. I get a CT scan in his office tomorrow afternoon. His scan will be used as the baseline for planning my radiation scheme, which will take seven to ten days to map out. Dr. Bonanno did affirm chemo is also warranted.

This particular cancer has no boundaries, so it can show up anywhere. (The NCI website calls it "insidious.") The chemo will kill those cells which have gotten out, but have not yet grown to where there is a viewable mass. Chemo will also make the cancer cells more susceptible to the radiation treatments. We need to pray that it makes the ones in the neck area very susceptible!

Judy and I will meet with the nutritionist tomorrow and I go back to the dental clinic on Friday for another consult. Monday we meet with the chemo oncologist, Dr. Prieto, on Eglin AFB to discuss that treatment regimen. Dr. Bonanno and

Dr. Prieto will then discuss how the chemo will fold into the radiation scheme, or vice versa.

As you can see, things are progressing. I fully expect to be in treatment within the next two weeks. From what I am gathering, this will be a process which will last about two months. Dr. Bonanno also re-emphasized there will be some "pain and burning" from the radiation. It is unavoidable, because of the large dose of radiation I will be receiving. He also said our best chance of killing the cancer is with this first effort, and I sense Dr. Bonanno will not under-utilize his resources in trying to kill the cancer, wherever it is. I can also expect to have lymph nodes in the neck—a couple, few, or all, TBD—removed sometime after we complete the radiation treatment. There is also a slight chance some might be removed before treatment begins. That, too, is to be determined very shortly.

Several have asked if I plan to continue to work while going through treatments. The answer is, I plan to work as long as is practical. From what I can gather (and imagine), it is likely, as I move into weeks three or four of treatment, that the cumulative effects of the chemo and radiation together will sap me of a lot of my strength and energy. There will also come a point, though I don't know when it will be, when my immune system is going to be severely weakened. That is just the nature of the treatments. When this occurs, it probably will not be smart to be out in public a lot. I am fortunate that I work for a company with good benefits, as well as good people up the chain who understand, and sympathize, with what is about to happen.

There are those addressed on this e-mail whom we haven't talked to for years. If you, or anyone else on here, want to chat at anytime, please let me know. I would very much enjoy re-establishing telephone contact.

Quite honestly, I wouldn't wish what we are experiencing on anyone, including my enemies, if I have any. However, if you had to experience something like this, you could not find a more wonderful group of people to endure it with than our church family in Destin, and our wonderful friends. Your friendship, concern, and prayers mean more than you can imagine. I will send another update Monday, after seeing the chemo oncologist. In the meantime, please continue to keep Judy and me in your prayers.

Don

P.S.: Please don't forget Dr. McMurphy in your prayers this week, as she undergoes her boards.

****

Our friends, Paula and Ray, accompanied us on this first visit with the Radiation Oncologist to both listen and help us ask questions where appropriate. (Ray also accompanied me on numerous other visits to my three doctors, and initially, to my chemo treatments, since we didn't know how I would respond to the chemo.) Since Ray had just finished radiation treatment for prostate cancer, he and Paula were well-versed in the routine and knew what was important for Judy and me to know.

As Dr. Bonnano accompanied us on our way out of the clinic, after the first appointment with him, Ray mentioned he had just finished radiation treatment for prostate cancer. Dr. Bonnano's response to him was, "You were lucky." Dr. Bonnano clearly meant my treatment would be far more difficult and painful than what Ray had experienced. That comment was very sobering.

Working, while being treated for base-of-tongue cancer, would have been just about impossible. Each morning's routine, after about the second week of treatment, was pretty lengthy. I had to wake up the mouth and clean it by rinsing and gargling with a salt water and baking soda solution. I had to brush my teeth with a prescription fluoride toothpaste and then wait thirty minutes before putting anything into the mouth. After that, there were pills to take and there would soon be another mouth treatment, which would take an hour to complete.

During the first couple of weeks of radiation and chemo, I was able to eat cereals and oat meal for breakfast. For reasons which will be explained later, I had to begin feeding myself through the feeding tube. Using the feeding tube actually helped speed up the morning routine, because I didn't have to wait the thirty minutes after brushing my teeth before having breakfast. As effects from the treatment began to compound, I wound up swishing with another medicine to treat the mouth sores. I then had to wait another hour after this treatment before putting anything in the mouth. The feeding tube was used at least four times a day to feed myself a concoction of Ensure, protein powder, honey, and milk. Then, in order to stay hydrated, I also had to pump 12-14 ounces of water or juices through the feeding tube, at least another four or five times a day. There were pills, such as Diflucan, for yeast in the mouth, as well as Zovirax, an anti-viral preventive. As it turned out, I was doing something in terms of body maintenance almost every thirty minutes each day, and I still had to make my scheduled doctor, chemo, and radiation appointments.

****

-----Original Message-----
From: Don Sublett
Sent: Monday, April 10, 7:49 PM
To: Support Group
Subject: Update #4

Dear Friends,

I think reality is beginning to catch up as we move closer to beginning treatments, on April 25th.

Last Wednesday, I went to 21st Century Radiation Oncology to get "prepped" for the start of radiation. The technician made me a bite block, which I will bite into during each treatment. The purpose is to get the tongue up and out of the way during treatments. He also made me a mask, which will keep my head and neck in the same position during each treatment. The mask reminded me of one of those nylon laundry bags you put your delicates in and throw in the washing machine. However, this mesh is stretched across a frame. It is heated and placed over the face. Then it is stretched down over the face/head and fastened to the bench. It will be tough to move when fastened to the bench, and that is good. They need me in the same position for each treatment as they try to be as precise in directing the radiation beams as possible. Treatments will last from five to fifteen minutes and I will likely be getting more than one radiation treatment each day.

Today, the "kid's gloves" came off when I met with the chemo oncologist on Eglin. That hour-long visit was undoubtedly the strongest dose of reality administered so far. Dr. Prieto was very straightforward with me as he outlined what I should expect as treatments progress. Whereas, Dr. Bonnano told me there will be some "pain and burning," Dr. Prieto told me things like, "Your throat will hurt so bad you won't want to swallow a tear." He also mentioned the pain would probably be so bad, "morphine will not kill it." Considering what I will most likely be contending with on the pain front, and the necessity to have good nutrition and hydration, we discussed whether or not to insert a feeding tube. I opted to have the tube inserted into the stomach, probably next week. It may not be needed, but it will be there if it is. Realistically, it is better to do it now, because doing it later might require a trachea, due to the condition of the mouth and throat. Also, there is no need for Judy to have to wrestle me in order to get food and liquids down me. My goal is to be a good patient.

I will be getting chemo weekly, during the course of radiation, and it looks like there will be six or seven chemo sessions. I was given the option of letting the nurse try to find a good vein each week, or to have a port inserted. For that reason, as well as a number of others, I will have a port inserted. Hopefully, the port and feeding tube can both be inserted during the same procedure.

I was mistaken in my belief regarding the function of the chemo. I thought it would seek out and kill any cancer cells which might be roaming free in the body. Evidently, this is not such a major concern (to them anyway). The chemo's function is to make the cancer cells in the neck and throat more susceptible to the radiation on a molecular level.

Toxicity will be a major concern. The cumulative effects of the "poison" that is being put into my body, as well as the radiation, will most likely cause significant problems. If I understood correctly, about 75% of patients have halts in their treatment due to toxicity. These effects will be felt almost immediately, and Dr. Prieto recommended I cease working when I begin treatment. I will most likely follow his recommendation.

There are two "reality battles" going on inside me right now. One battle says, "You have a really serious condition which is going to change you dramatically, and that change is (really) going to start in a couple of weeks." The other battle says, "You are healthy. You don't hurt. You are still able to do everything you have been doing. Maybe this is a bad dream." Both are true, except for the fact this isn't a dream. I do have this cancer which has to be dealt with, and I am, fortunately, in good health. The latter should stand me in good stead as I try to be one of the 25% who makes it through without any halts. Halting treatment only detracts from the overall effectiveness of the regimen. If I am going to have to endure this—and I am—then I want maximum effectiveness.

As we get closer to the start of treatments, it is becoming more obvious there will be some difficult times ahead. I am smart enough to realize this is not something I can do on my own. It is nice to have the confidence we enjoy in knowing we have God on our side, and that you are also supporting us with your love, concern, help, and prayers.

In Christian Love,

Don

Of all the preparations involved in getting ready to begin treatment for my cancer, having the feeding tube inserted was unquestionably the smartest thing I did. I wound up having to use the feeding tube considerably sooner than I anticipated and it was a blessing the tube was in place. If you, or anyone you know, is going to have radiation administered to the head or neck, *strongly* encourage them to have a feeding tube inserted. Many oncologists will insist on it, but others will not be nearly as adamant.

In my case, Dr. Prieto said he used to be one-hundred-percent adamant that any patient who was being treated for a head-and-neck cancer would have a feeding tube, or he would not treat them. However, Dr. Prieto said he had somewhat relaxed that viewpoint over the years and was only about ninety-five-percent insistent on it, now. I commented that I didn't know if I would be a hero or a wimp, but if I had to guess, I would probably be a wimp. In that case, Dr. Prieto said I might want to seriously consider getting a feeding tube. Ray—who had accompanied me—and I looked at each other and gave each other a north/south nod. Best move I made!

While I was undergoing chemo, Dr. Prieto's oncology nurse, Phyllis Bernier, attended an oncology nurse's convention up in the northeast. She came back and advised that the thinking among a large number of the doctors, now, was to not permit their head-and-neck cancer patients to have a feeding tube inserted when undergoing treatment. There had been a patient who had contracted pneumonia from not exercising the neck and throat muscles, and died. Thus, they thought it best to forego the feeding tube in order to keep this from occurring again. I think this approach is akin to "throwing the baby out with the bath water"! None of these doctors, obviously, have ever been treated for cancer in the head or neck, and are ignorant of what they proposed. If the doctor says no to a feeding tube, find another doctor immediately!

****

-----Original Message-----
From: Sanford Flach
Sent: Wednesday, April 12, 3:22 PM
To: Don Sublett
Subject: Received update #4

Hi Don,

I received update #4 from a lady at church. Glad to hear you are rapidly progressing toward getting some treatment. I went through all of the prep work you described, except the bite block and the feeding tube. The feeding tube was discussed as something they would do, if necessary. In my case, I would have welcomed one the last week of my treatment, but since I had gone that far without it, they gave me a morphine elixir and I toughed it out through my final few treatments. I had radiation twice a day for almost eight weeks. I only had chemo three times. During the latter part of my treatments, I drank several Ensure each day. I also drank pure fresh-squeezed carrot juice during the early part of my treatment.

We bought a juicer and we juiced five pounds of carrots at a time. Fresh carrot juice is actually very good, but as my treatment progressed and the soreness of my throat became worse, it hurt too much to drink it. I need to get back on the fresh carrot juice, now that I am better, as it is extremely high on the list of things which can heal you and keep you healthy. They never mentioned the possibility of delaying any treatments until the last couple of days, as they all remarked about how well I was doing in hanging in there and not delaying any treatments. Up until then, I never thought there was an option for retreat.

Looking back, I am glad I kept on with my treatment, regardless of the pain it caused. As your treatments progress, you will need to eat more food that has been pureed. One thing I enjoyed eating was yogurt. During the course of my treatments, I lost between 40 and 50 pounds. I will admit that I did need to lose about 30-40 pounds, but now I have gained about ten pounds back and I want to try to maintain my current weight. I had been drinking skim milk for the past 35 years and eating very little margarine, but my doctor advised me to switch to whole milk and eat real butter and anything else that might help me fight the weight loss.

On the advice of one of my chemo nurses, I started drinking 100% grape juice and eating baked sweet potatoes. During the mid-to-late part of my treatments, my blood count was often too low to receive my chemo, even with them giving me the shots which are supposed to bring it up. Believe it or not, drinking and eating the above items did, in fact, help. I tried to eat at least one sweet potato every day, and I drank at least one glass of grape juice each day, thereafter.

Hang in there and keep a positive attitude! You will get better and soon, this cancer thing will be a thing in the past!

We will continue to keep you in our prayers.

Sanford

-----Original Message-----
From: Don Sublett
Sent: Wednesday, April 12, 9:37 PM
To: Sanford Flach
Subject: Received update #4

Sanford,

I really appreciate hearing from you. In fact, the thought to call you has crossed my mind a couple of times. I mentioned to Gilda, Sunday, at church, that you called and she was thrilled you had.

I thought you mentioned you had three chemo treatments. I am not sure why my regimen is different, but it obviously is, or planned to be, if I can tolerate it. I, too, will get the Cisplatin. The doctor went over a couple other chemicals they sometimes use and seemed to rule them out, saying he felt the platinum chemotherapy drug was the best for my cancer.

I am surprised to learn you drank a lot of carrot juice. I assume that has beta carotene in it, and beta carotene is the one thing the doctor advised me against consuming. I will mention your comment to him at my next appointment. However, I will take your advice on the yogurt, and grape juice. We will stock up on the Ensure and add some non-fat milk and protein powder to it. I expect to consume quite a few Dairy Queen milk shakes, yogurt smoothies, etc., toward the end of treatment, too. I weigh 185 and could probably stand to drop a few pounds, but don't believe Dr. Prieto will tolerate much weight loss, according to his nurse.

I certainly don't want a break in my treatments, as painful as they might be. While I am not looking forward to the treatments, I am looking forward to getting them behind me. I know there are a lot of medicines which will be available to make it as bearable as possible and I expect to have to use quite a number of them. Makes you appreciate modern chemistry, huh?

I have added you to my update list. I probably will not have another update until I get the port and feeding tube in, or maybe not until the day before treatments actually begin. Will be wanting a lot of prayer at that time, and on through the end. Certainly appreciate the way you have reached out and shared your experience!

Kind regards,

Don

I had spoken with Sanford a couple times before our e-mail exchange above, and it was good to have an idea of what I was in store for. Our treatment regimens were considerably different, but the treatment side-effects were expected to likely be very similar.

****

-----Original Message-----
From: Don Sublett
Sent: Tuesday, April 18, 4:54 PM
To: Support Group
Subject: Update #5

Dear Friends,

Momentum is increasing and reality is fast approaching. In fact, I expect reality will wind up taped to my stomach Thursday afternoon, in the form of a feeding tube.

I met, Monday, with a surgeon in the Eglin Surgery Clinic. He will insert the Medi-Port (for chemo) and the feeding tube on Thursday. I will then be admitted overnight for observation. This hospital stay will "trigger" my Short-Term Disability Leave (STDL) from work. My chemo oncologist expects me to be out of work for approximately sixteen weeks: eight weeks treatment and at least eight weeks for recovery. This could vary, depending on the length of treatment and my response to it. One nice twist with the STDL is that I can supplement it with two days vacation time each week and continue to draw full salary during my absence from work.

We met, today, with the nurse who will administer my chemo treatments. The reason I use the plural is I will be getting two courses of chemo each week. Surprise! I will be getting Cisplatin on Wednesday and Docetaxol on Thursday. Dr. Prieto went back and reviewed some literature on my particular type of cancer and on-going clinical trials indicate a better response from the combined "poisons." Though these will be "low dose" chemo regimens, they will still be potent enough to cause the usual side-effects: decrease in blood cell and platelet counts, fatigue, and numerous other potential side-effects I will not bother you with. I will also be getting anti-nausea drugs, steroids, and probably some other "stuff" I don't recall, in the chemo drips.

I am cautioned against eating out in restaurants, because of the chance of eating something undercooked or not properly cleaned. You can imagine Judy's response to that! We are also cautioned against being out in large crowds. Ray, who has been at virtually every appointment with us, asked specifically about attending church. The nurse didn't say, "Don't go," but she did seem a little squeamish at the thought of being exposed to such a large number of people. As my blood count and immune defenses drop, I will become increasingly susceptible to infection. Though the infections can be fought, catching one may cause my treatment to have to be halted. That, we don't want. So, if we do attend services, it is likely we will be sitting in the back and will probably duck out pretty quickly.

I just had to call 21st Century Radiation Oncology today and ask about my radiation regimen! The suspense of not knowing—especially after learning of the double chemo treatment—just what to expect, was getting to me. I am in contact with two other men who had cancer in the base of the tongue and they each had radiation treatments twice a day, so I naturally expected the same thing. However, I am scheduled for only one radiation session a day over a period of about eight weeks. I don't know if that means I get a double dose each day or what. I expect there is not much slack being cut for me in the overall dosage.

There have been some other things going on over the course of the last week. The kids and grandkids spent a few days with us. It was an enjoyable time, in spite of this cancer cloud hanging over us. We all needed to sit down together and discuss my cancer, the treatments, and develop a plan for coping with the demands the treatments will place upon us, particularly Judy. Either Leslie, or Michael (our daughter and son), will be here with us to help out the last three or four weeks of treatments. It is also likely this help will need to be extended for a couple weeks after radiation and chemo cease. I will be at the weakest point then, though recovery will be starting.

I also met with Elders/Shepherds of the congregation, last Tuesday evening, and they anointed me with oil and prayed for me. *I believe in the power of prayer* and can offer no explanation other than answered prayer for the lack of fear as we move forward with the treatments. I obviously have some trepidation about the amount of pain and discomfort I will experience, and how I will respond. That is why I have concern for Judy. She is the one who will have to deal with me in whatever way I respond. She needs your prayers and help, too.

This cancer is most certainly life-threatening, but it is not an immediate death sentence. Not everyone is so fortunate. It is treatable and I have every confidence I will be cured. If that is not the case, as Ray and I discussed after the first appointment with the radiation oncologist, when Dr. Bonnano said, "The survival rate is 60-70 percent, but I can't tell you which side you will come down on." Ray said, "I didn't want to argue with the doctor, but I know which side you will come down on. It is the side of life!" It is nice to have that assurance.

Several have confided they didn't know if they would respond like I have, under the same circumstances. I believe you would likely respond in a similar fashion. Quite simply, you will either fight, or give in to the disease and die. I believe God gave us the instinct to fight as hard as possible and the capacity to endure whatever we must in order to overcome things like cancer. I never imagined myself in this situation. I was just going to die peacefully in my sleep at about the age of 95, just like you, but I now know that may not be quite how it happens. However, I certainly appreciate the fact God is on my side.

Finally, (I realize this is somewhat lengthy), we really appreciate the e-mails, calls, cards, letters, and *prayers* for us. You have no idea unless you've been here—and some addressed here have—what strength and encouragement is gained through those expressions of concern, support, and love. It is so overwhelming, but also, so humbling to know that you care.

We love and appreciate you so very much!

Judy and Don

****

-----Original Message-----
From: Don Sublett
Sent: Friday, April 21, 12:18 PM
To: Support Group
Subject: Update #6

Hi, Everyone!

This is short in order to make up for the last one.

I am home from the hospital after having the feeding tube and chemo port inserted. I am doing well—a bit sore, but the doctor said this morning I earned the soreness. Lest anyone should wonder, they still come around every four hours during the night to make sure you're sleeping (not so well) and to take your vitals. Nothing has changed since I was last in the hospital overnight, in about 1993.

Yesterday was both interesting and challenging. We stopped by the ER to see if they would check Judy's rough cough she's had off and on for a month. Not wanting to abuse the system, I explained what was in store for me and that we were trying to keep her from having to go to Hurlburt to see our Primary Care doctor, in the midst of all of this. They were not busy and said, "Sure, we will take a look at her." That response is so typical of everyone we encounter at the hospital!

To make a long story short, Judy had a fever and bronchitis. So, they kept Judy in the ER, giving her an IV and meds through the IV. She finally got up to my room, after I came back from surgery, in much better condition than when I left her. Fortunately, our "good shadows," Paula and Ray, were there and Paula attended to Judy, while Ray attended to me. We also had help from Brad, one of our ministers. We certainly appreciate their being there! Sometimes, your cup gets kinda full, if you know what I mean.

My next major milestone is the dry run, on Monday, for radiation. That is to make sure all their measurements and alignments are accurate. Then, radiation and a first chemo treatment will be given on Tuesday, instead of Wednesday. For a reason I am unaware of, the Docetaxel has to be given with the radiation. At that point, we start to kill these cancer cells. I am ready.

I will never quit saying it; we appreciate your love, concern, and prayers!

Don

Having friends who can attend appointments with you is a genuine blessing, especially if they have experienced something similar to what you are going through. They can really take a load off your mind, as well as provide valuable insight into what you will likely experience. Paula and Ray latched onto us at the initial diagnosis of my cancer and never turned loose. We also had many generous offers of help from an incredible number of people and would have used them, if circumstances had warranted.

-----Original Message-----
From: Pat Rice
Sent: Monday, April 24, 5:59 AM
To: Don Sublett
Subject: Update #6

Dear Don,

It isn't that I haven't been thinking about you and Judy. And it isn't that I don't have you both in my prayers every day. What it is, is I just can't seem to find the words to express to you how sorry I am about your present plight. Would that it were not so. Having read each of your updates, I marvel at the coolness with which you describe the unfolding horrible things you have to look forward to. You are letting us participate with you by these updates, even though we are sitting in the bleachers; but you must know we are praying for you and cheering for you every day. I experienced some of these things with Jeep, but his cancer was not painful, and at least, not difficult to treat. Even his chemo didn't have drastic side-effects. I pray that the doctors were giving you a "worst case scenario" and that their severe predictions will be less than they have led you to believe. My prayer is that God, through His Mighty Power, will deliver you from this cancer and make you well again.

In Christian love,

Pat

-----Original Message-----
From: Don Sublett
Sent: Monday, April 24, 4:02 PM
To: Pat Rice
Subject: Update #6

Pat,

You are a sweet, sweet lady. Judy and I both deeply appreciate your concerns, and most certainly, your prayers. We, too, are sorry about the situation, but we need to channel whatever energies might be spent worrying toward overcoming the effects of the treatments. I really believe God is hearing and answering prayers on our behalf, already; but there is probably no way to avoid the pain of the radiation, short of being in a coma. The doctor has already said he will not do that. Ha!

I believe the doctors are presenting a most-likely case scenario. It tracks pretty closely with what I have been told by the two men I know who have also had the same cancer. My doctors will use whatever medications are available to help ease the effects, but there will be no way around the "burning" of the throat area. We will just have to tough our way through it. I know it is easy to sit here and type those words, because I am not there yet. I don't know how I will respond, but I hope it is not in an unkind way.

Cancer doesn't have to hurt and that is why it is so insidious. You seldom, anymore, see those promos about cancer being the "silent killer." That is a shame, because it really is. That is why we need to pay attention to what is going on in our body.

I will do another update this evening to bring folks up to speed, but just wanted to say, "Thank you." for your kindness and concern.

Don

****

The evening after I got home from having the Medi-port and feeding tube inserted, Judy came in from school both feeling and looking miserable. So, we took her to the Eglin Emergency Room. The ER doctor diagnosed Judy with pneumonia and spent several hours giving her antibiotics and breathing treatments to try and get her oxygen absorption rate up to acceptable levels, but was not able to make that happen.

While they were working on Judy, we told the staff I had cancer and had just had the Medi-port and feeding tube inserted. As we were waiting for them to admit Judy to the ward, I realized it was time to have the dressing over the feeding tube changed.

Admittedly, I was a little squeamish at tackling the bandage change for the first time. So, I asked the nurse who had been attending to Judy if she would be so kind as to do the first dressing change for me. The nurse said she didn't mind at all.

She got some gauze bandages, tape, and Betadine, and had me sit on one of the rolling stools. She removed the dressing, and as I looked for the first time at the tube sticking out of my stomach, it got *real hot* in the cubicle. I started fading and began sliding off of the stool. It was a memorable moment, as she tried to keep me from sliding off that rolling stool while hollering for some help!

Help arrived and we all had a pretty good laugh...after it started to cool off. The nurse got the wound cleaned, changed the dressing, and managed to "find" me a bed next to my wife, there in the ER.

Even though I knew the feeding tube was there, seeing it sticking out of my stomach was a genuine reality check. It rocked me to my core.

-----Original Message-----
From: Don Sublett
Sent: Monday, April 24, 7:04 PM
To: Support Group
Subject: Update #7

Hi, Everyone!

I hadn't decided if I would provide an update today, but many realized today would be a pretty important day and I have gotten three calls asking if there would be one. So, I will try to make this one short, as well.

First, we got Judy home today after four days in the Eglin Hospital, recovering from pneumonia. We are thankful that her health is returning just as mine is likely to be going the other way for a while. Tomorrow we begin killing the cancer cells. I have chemo scheduled for 12:30 P.M., Tuesday and Wednesday, and radiation at 3:10 P.M. each day this week, except for Friday, at 10:30 A.M. Chemo will continue twice weekly and radiation will be Mon.-Fri. None on weekends or holidays.

We met, today, with just about everyone who will be involved in my treatments over the next several weeks. The radiation techs strapped me to the linear accelerator to check the alignment, and tattooed my neck (just a tiny one). Dr. Prieto discussed the chemo regimen, once again, and Phyllis (his nurse, who will administer the chemo) also went over her procedures. It looks like we are all in sync.

A couple good things came out of today's visits: (1) it appears treatments will be over 35 treatment days; they have me on the books for 55 radiation treatments over a period of 35 treatment days. Dr. McMurphy was right in her initial assessment of how long the treatment period would be. And (2) chemo may not be so severe as to be the cause of the drop in blood cell/platelet counts. However, that is not to minimize the effects of the chemo. The chemo oncologist's concern is the radiation treatments may not be tolerable and might have to be halted for a period. I thought the chemo would be a significant driver in the possible halt of treatments, but Dr. Prieto doesn't believe chemo will be a factor. Chemo is "low dose." As long as I am getting radiation, I will get chemo. Radiation oncology will be the determiner of whether treatments continue, or are halted.

It is almost hard to believe it was a month ago, today, that the diagnosis was confirmed. It has been an eventful month, and that is an understatement. However, even with the feeding tube and the chemo port, it still doesn't quite seem real yet. That will undoubtedly change tomorrow, as we get very proactive in the start of killing these cancer cells before they kill me. As we start to ratchet-up the treatment, I ask that you also begin to ratchet-up your prayers for both Judy and I.

In Christian Love,

Don

My radiation treatment plan and record were contained in a three-inch binder. Daily treatments, doctor exams, and other information was recorded and maintained in that binder. It also contained a printout of where, and how deep, the radiation would be projected during each of the eight stops the linear accelerator would make as it rotated around my body.

As we were getting ready to start treatment, one of the technicians offered to show me what my plan looked like. They had taken the CT scan, which showed the tumor locations and structure of the jaw, neck, and spine, and overlaid projections of how the radiation would strike each of the tumors from each of the eight stops. I was impressed by the accuracy and precision with which they could work. I could see clearly how they planned to avoid the spinal cord. Seeing this visual depiction of the radiation, I was curious and asked whether they radiated a specific area, or a region. I was told they hit the region where the tumor is located, but also shoot (radiate) a one centimeter border—about four-tenths of an inch—around the area of the tumor.

As precise as my treatment plan was, I was told that in about three months they would be able to be even more precise. They would be upgrading their technology with a machine which would enable them to "see" the tumor with one machine and "shoot" it with another. As I prepared to begin treatments, I got a lot of "help" in the form of suggestions about how to kill the cancer. Since my e-mails had been spread far and wide to people I had no knowledge of, I probably got more suggestions than some might. There were people who suggested I stop my approach immediately and see a doctor they recommended. Others suggested I take a holistic approach and let the body heal itself. There were suggestions of a vegetarian diet without the use of chemo, and I also had one suggestion that I go on a raw meat diet.

I have to believe all who offered help were genuinely sincere in their belief that the approach they suggested would be effective in killing my cancer. However, I have tremendous faith in modern medicine, so I responded to each that, while I was sure they were sincere and I appreciated their suggestion, I had determined what my course of treatment would be and was pressing ahead with it. I also asked them to please continue to keep me in their prayers.

-----Original Message-----
From: Larry Lewis
Sent: Monday, April 24, 6:59 PM
To: Don Sublett
Subject: Re: Update #7

Don,

My sister-in-law, in PA., had a neighbor with a very similar diagnosis. Treatment is a bear, but she recovered fully and that has been a couple years ago. We will go fishing again after you feel better, but I may have to do the eight-hour trip this time.

Larry

-----Original Message-----
From: Don Sublett
Sent: Monday, April 24, 8:07 PM
To: Larry Lewis
Subject: Re: Update #7

Larry,

This type of cancer does respond well to treatment. As you say, the treatment will be a bear. The alternative is to give in and die. I realize I will die sometime, but I am not ready to give in yet. Though it is possible, I might wish that would happen before we get done with this. They will be giving me morphine patches, probably starting at 25mg and boosting it up to 100mg toward the end. The doctor says that will make the pain bearable, but will not kill it. I have a hard time imagining that, but expect to soon feel it. Hopefully, not for an interminable period.

Sure need the prayers to get through this.

Don

-----Original Message-----
From: Rick W.
Sent: Monday, April 24, 8:34 PM
To: Don Sublett
Subject: RE: Update #6

Don,

Good luck tomorrow. We miss you out here.
Not having a running buddy is not any fun! Our
thoughts are with you (especially tomorrow).

Rick

-----Original Message-----
From: Don Sublett
Sent: Monday, April 24, 7:47 AM
To: Rick W.
Subject: RE: Update #6

Thanks, Rick.

As Curt told me, *"Fight's On!!!"* I have made
that call before, but never like this.

Don

The day before I began treatments, our team headed back to Nellis AFB to conduct the final phase of the experiment we had been helping plan for the past two years. This was our sixth experiment and it was the first time one of us had not been able to participate in one of the events. Needless to say, I would have much rather been at Nellis AFB working than having to undergo cancer treatments.

What makes our nation's fighter pilots the best in the world is quality training, along with superior aircraft and weapons engineering. One aspect of that training is their preparation for air-to-air combat. Our fighter aircrews engage in a building block training process called Air Combat Training (ACT). ACT involves flying and fighting against similar airframes—F-16 versus F-16. Young aircrews will begin with one versus one and build-up from there. Dissimilar Air Combat Training (DACT) involves flying and fighting against different aircraft—F-15 versus F-22—again, starting with 1v1 and building on the numbers and complexity of the mission from that point. Each type of training usually occurs within well-defined military operating areas (MOAs) and restricted airspace.

For part of my Air Force career, my job was to sit at a radar scope in a Command and Control facility and provide intercept control and advisories to fighters participating in ACT/DACT.

When readying for a fight, the aircrews marshal to their distant part of the airspace and get set to begin the engagement. They'll look at cloud conditions, contrails level and sun angle to optimize their advantage. Once ready to fight, the flight lead advises his/her flight controller. Coordination occurs between the two controllers sitting adjacent and the engagement begins with a *"Fight's On!!!"* call. This call to begin the fight gets the adrenalin and competitive juices flowing!

A typical initial transmission to begin the engagement would be: *"Fight's On!!!* Raptor 21 Flight, Kill (Mission), One-Three-Zero (Bearing), Sixty-Five (Range in miles), Twenty-Eight Thousand (Altitude)." From there, controllers provide timely updates until the engagement is completed, training objectives are met, and/ or simulated kills are achieved.

Upon completion, the call to *"Knock It Off!!!"* is made, followed by participants deconflicting from each other, checking fuel states, and heading back to their respective corners of the airspace to begin another engagement.

-----Original Message-----
From: Dave and Leslie Miller
Sent: Monday, April 24, 9:13 PM
To: Don Sublett
Subject: Re: Update #7

Dad,

Thanks, once again, for taking the time to write an update. I am so glad Mom was able to come home today. I know that will simplify things this week and eliminate some stress for all of us. I keep telling her she must take it easy this week, but I am not sure she is listening. Please keep an eye on her and don't let her do more than she can handle. (I can just see her painting the garage floor because she has the week off!)

Good luck tomorrow. I have to say, I am glad the time has come to begin treatment. I just want to get this underway before more cells have time to spread. Please know we are praying for you and so are *many* of our friends. God will get us through this. I have no doubt. Let me know if I am needed down there and I will be on the next plane headed south, out of Reagan National Airport.

Talk to you tomorrow evening. We have an event at Lauren's school tomorrow night, at 7:00, so I will call before we leave.

Love,

Leslie

-----Original Message-----
From: Don Sublett
Sent: Monday, April 24, 8:07 PM
To: Dave and Leslie Miller
Subject: Re: Update #7

Les,

Yes, it was good to get mom home. I think she will take it easy this week. She knows what is at stake.

The doc, today, seemed to indicate the three weeks after treatment will not be any fun, either. So, we may need to look at some help from you all through about the 4th of July week, to the extent that you can. We realize you all have lives, and in Michael's case, unlike you with the summer off, a job. Not to mention limited vacation. We will just have to see how things flow out, but my care for three or four weeks may pretty much be a full-time proposition. Might even need some muscle to get me into the car to (force me to) go to treatments. Ha!

Love you all,

Dad

-----Original Message-----
From: Cathy Mosley
Sent: Tuesday, April 25, 11:12 AM
To: Don Sublett
Subject: Re: Update #7

Hi Mr. Sublett,

My family and I are new members at the Destin Church of Christ. I wanted to thank you for the detailed e-mails you are sending out. I am a detailed prayer warrior and like to be as specific as I can when I go to our Lord with requests. Jimmy and I have had you and your wife in our prayers since we first heard your news. We look forward to witnessing your healing and pray for no halt in your treatments. We are so glad to hear that Mrs. Sublett is back home and getting better. May God bless you both.

In His love,

Cathy

-----Original Message-----
From: Don Sublett
Sent: Tuesday, April 25, 5:36 PM
To: Cathy Mosley
Subject: Re: Update #7

Cathy,

    We do love having dedicated prayer warriors reaching out to God on our behalf! I, literally, can't tell you what that means to us. Judy and I look forward to getting better acquainted with you and your family, and thanking you personally for your love and concern. Our Destin family is such a blessing to us!

    Don

III.

"FIGHT'S ON!!!": Killing the Cancer

-----Original Message-----
From: Don Sublett
Sent: Tuesday, April 25, 9:02 PM
To: Support Group
Subject: Update #8

Good Evening Everyone,

This will probably be my last update for a while. Now that I am in treatment, the routine will be pretty stable and the only thing which will happen is the effects will increase over time. Around weeks three or four, if not sooner, the pain will begin to get very intense and I expect to be on some pretty heavy doses of morphine. Sanford, over in Mobile, told me he began with 25mg morphine patches and worked his way up to 100mg. He then tapered off in the weeks after treatments ended. Walt, here in Destin, also had some heavy duty pain medicines, especially at the end.

Yesterday, when I described to Dr. Prieto what I had been told, he concurred. Dr. Prieto also said they were very liberal with the pain meds, including the narcotics. As previously mentioned to some, he again emphasized that, while the pain would not be deadened, it will be made tolerable. I like the fact that punches are not being pulled with me. From my perspective, it will be far better to be the beneficiary of answered prayer and things not be as severe as what I am being told, than to be blindsided by the harshness of the cumulative effects. I don't know that I can adequately prepare mentally, but with your prayers and God's help, I can try.

My doctors are also concerned with minimizing the side effects in other areas. For example, I was given four different meds: steroids, anti-itch, anti-nausea, and one I can't recall at the moment, prior to the Docetaxel, today. As I sit here, it seems those meds have worked their magic. I was also given a topical numbing ointment to apply to the skin over the chemo port 90 minutes before my appointment. As a result, I hardly felt the stick. Clearly, there is better living through chemistry. I encourage everyone to hug a chemist!

While I am still pretty clear-headed, I want to tell you once again that your cards, letters, phone calls, visits, offers of help, and your *prayers* mean more than I can adequately express. We will be accepting some of those offers of help, especially to drive me to some of my treatments the next three weeks. After that, there will be other family members here to help Judy in caring for me.

Many of you have forwarded these messages around the world: Alaska, Germany, Afghanistan, Iraq, England, and God knows where else. We do appreciate that word of the need for prayer has spread so far and wide—and so many have answered the call! It is really a joy to go to the mailbox each day and to sit down before the computer to check e-mail. I have tried to respond to each e-mail. If I haven't, it is clearly an oversight and not an intended slight. I have yet to delete a message which has been received and may never do so.

Finally, I don't know if we killed any cancer cells today. If not, they were given notice that, as one of my co-workers, Curt, mentioned in an e-mail last night, clearly...

"Fight's On!!!"

Don

Previously, I was well away from the engagement, and often in a semi-hardened command and control facility, or a radar van, both of which were well out of the direct line of fire. As we began killing cancer cells, the *"Fight's On!!!"* call was a very real and personal call, because I was more a part of the fight than I had ever been before. Something was going to die and I certainly did not want it to be me!

-----Original Message-----
From: John Fuhrmann
Sent: Wednesday, April 26, 5:25 AM
To: Don Sublett
Subject: Re: Update #8

Game's on! Don and Judy.

Serve hard, hit roll-outs, and hang on to your smiles. Prayers and thoughts from Erie, PA.

John & Bette

-----Original Message-----
From: Don Sublett

Sent: Wednesday, April 26, 8:16 AM
To: John Fuhrmann
Subject: Re: Update #8

John and Bette,

You are ever-so correct! I have made the *"Fight's On!!!"* call numerous times and always got fired up when doing it, *never* expecting to lose. That is the way I feel this time, too. Only, before, I was pretty safe, many miles from where the engagements were taking place. This time is most certainly different, because I am the target.

I have good doctors, the best technology available, lots of prayer, and God's help in pulling through this. It will most likely get pretty tough, but we will take it one day at a time when it does. There is a finite number of treatments, so there is an end in sight, always. I will be constantly reminded of that.

Thanks for your support in helping us get through this.

Don

John and I have known each other for well over twenty-five years. We first met on the racquetball court at Griffiss AFB, NY. John is a highly skilled racquetball player and also was an exceptional fighter pilot. The "roll-out" racquetball shot is the perfect, unreturnable shot. It hits the bottom of the front wall and the floor right in the crack, and rolls out without a bounce. If I ever needed to hit a "roll-out," now was the time.

-----Original Message-----
From: Yvonne Borlinghaus
Sent: Wednesday, April 26, 7:15 AM
To: Don Sublett
Subject: Re: Update #8

So good to "hear" from you. Trust me, your bravery and attitude are more uplifting to us than we to you. The prayers, thoughts, and love will continue throughout this ordeal. Wish we could all take just a little of the pain from you and kind of spread it out a bit, but that just isn't the way it works. Hang in there and call us anytime. Love you,

Yvonne

-----Original Message-----
From: Don Sublett
Sent: Wednesday, April 26, 8:28 AM
To: Yvonne Borlinghaus
Subject: Re: Update #8

Yvonne,

It is pretty easy right now, because there is no pain. However, when it does begin to hit, I am certain it will be far less than it would have been without all the prayers and God's intervention. I can't imagine what folks without that prayer pipeline have to endure.

Looking forward to seeing you all and sure appreciate your willingness to come help us out. I feel like Judy will really need the support, as will I.

We love you all.

Don

-----Original Message-----
From: Gilda Laird
Sent: Wednesday, April 26, 7:49 AM
To: Don Sublett
Subject: Re: Update #8

Don, you were in my constant thoughts and prayers yesterday as you started down the road of healing. It seemed every time I had a minute to breathe at work, your name came to mind. So, I took that as a sign to offer up another prayer on your behalf. Your courage, faith, and absolute trust in what God has laid before you is, and will continue to be, a source of encouragement to me. You have "spurred me on" and I can only hope, and pray, that if I face something like this, I will have the courage, faith, and trust in God that you have shown. Chip and I want to be of help to you and Judy and we will be calling to see what we can do, whether it be to sit with you while Judy goes out, or mow the lawn. I love you, Don!

Gilda

-----Original Message-----
From: Don Sublett
Sent: Wednesday, April 26, 9:07 AM
To: Gilda Laird
Subject: Re: Update #8

Gilda,

You are so kind and thoughtful! The prayers are appreciated more than you might imagine. I know there will be some difficult days ahead, but they will be made easier because of answered prayer. I expect the vast majority of the Christian family we know would respond in pretty much the same way I have. What is the point in having a faith in God if you are not going to trust in and lean on Him during life's most difficult struggles? We know He is there for us, and is the greatest resource we have. I pity those who don't have that hope and trust in Him. This has made me more aware of the need to reach out, and I plan to.

We will likely need some help along the way, but I don't know what form it will take. It is nice to know there are people wanting to help out where they can. We certainly appreciate, and love, you and Chip!

Don

-----Original Message-----
From: Walt Leirer
Sent: Wednesday, April 26, 8:18 AM
To: Don Sublett
Subject: Re: Update #8

Good Morning Don,

You keeping your e-mail is like I have done. I have kept all my cards and letters from when I was sick. I have gone through them and tried to throw them away, but just have not been able to yet. It will be five years on May 1st.

What was surprising was, after I was out of danger and back to my senses, I found out how far-spread around the world prayers were being offered up for me. I was so surprised at the different faiths and parts of the country and the world. It just blew me away! *God is love* and he loves you, and me. I guess that is why.

Your brother in Christ,

Walt

-----Original Message-----
From: Don Sublett
Sent: Wednesday, April 26, 9:22 AM
To: Walt Leirer
Subject: Re: Update #8

Walt,

My sister just told me a church in South Africa is also praying for me. Word has certainly spread far and wide.

Got one treatment day down and thirty-four to go. Wasn't going to count the treatment days, but it may be impossible not to. Thanks for sharing your experiences with me.

Don

-----Original Message-----
From: Skip Morgan
Sent: Wednesday, April 26, 9:36 AM
To: Don Sublett
Subject: Re: Update #8

Cousin Don,

I have been following your e-mails concerning your condition. I want you to know I go out into the woods almost every day to pray for you. I have not e-mailed you before, as I know how hard this is on you and your family. You do not need to reply. I just wanted you to know I think of you often and pray for you each day. I remember the good visits we had as young boys. I miss your Mom and Dad.

Skip

-----Original Message-----
From: Don Sublett
Sent: Wednesday, April 26, 11:55 AM
To: Skip Morgan
Subject: Re: Update #8

Skip,

It is good to hear from you. It is a shame we haven't kept in closer contact over the years. The times we spent together as kids were really great and a source of fond memories as I look back at some of those times now. However, we grow up, acquire obligations, and take on life's challenges. You have had a cross to bear over the years and I admire the way you never seemed to let it get the best of you. Now, I have a serious challenge ahead of *me*.

Yes, the cancer diagnosis was quite a blow—actually a *stunner*—but, after a day or two, we came to grips with what lay before us. I am confident I will be cured and I am also certain the cure is going to be quite painful, but it will be made tolerable through the use of morphine patches and some other chemical magic. The killing effects of the chemo and radiation will continue for three to six weeks after treatments cease. Looking at the calendar, things should start to slack up for me around July 4th. That is when the actual healing from the treatments should kick in pretty solidly.

Judy and I certainly appreciate the power of prayer and love knowing there are so many lifting us up before God. I am certain it is those prayers which have enabled us to get to this point with minimal emotional sorrow. We have had some down moments, but there have certainly been more up ones. I hope that continues as we get closer to where I will start to feel the effects of the treatments.

Please continue to pray for us. I know you will. Perhaps, after we get this behind us, we will be able to get together. If you have never seen this part of Florida, it is truly beautiful.

Again, thanks for making contact and remembering us in prayer. You are on my prayer list now, as well!

Don

-----Original Message-----
From: Dub Stearn
Sent: Wednesday, April 26, 2:20 PM
To: Don Sublett
Subject: Re: Update #8

Don,

We must all find the silver lining in all our challenges and this has improved my prayer time with the Father. As I said earlier, you are a constant reminder for me to lift you up so, while I pray for you, I figure it is a great time to put *all* things before Him. Before I know it, I have had an awesome time with God! I am able to be lifted up with our conversation. Thanks Don.

You're in my prayers,

Dub

-----Original Message-----
From: Don Sublett
Sent: Wednesday, April 26, 3:48 PM
To: Dub Stearn
Subject: Re: Update #8

Dub,

I am finding myself in a bit more constant communication with God than in times past. I am certainly more aware of the power He has in my life. Judy and I really love and appreciate our Destin family, and the love and support being provided to us. Don't know what we would do without it.

We love you all!

Don

-----Original Message-----
From: Marilyn Jones
Sent: Monday, May 01, 2006 12:23 PM
To: Don Sublett
Subject: Re: Update #8

Dear Don,

I am glad to hear Judy is up and going, and I assume, probably at work today. Jerry is still on his motorcycle trip. He has never been sick and, after some tests, was told he had the good body health of a man in his 20s. He acquired good genes for wellness and long life. Many of his cousins and some other family members have lived into their 90s. We will see if the good health holds for him. He has walked away from airplane and motorcycle accidents that should have killed him.

Still praying for you every morning, just for that day.

Love,

Marilyn

-----Original Message-----
From: Don Sublett
Sent: Monday, May 01, 5:46 PM
To: Marilyn Jones
Subject: Re: Update #8

Marilyn,

It is a shame that it takes something like cancer to reconnect with many people from times past, but that part of this experience has been especially enjoyable. As you suspected, Judy did work today. In fact, she just walked in the door. The woman was born to teach and dearly loves it. "Teacher of the Year" for two of the last three years. Kids love her!

I am sure Jerry is enjoying his trip. I have a good friend over in Panama City who still rides his Harley and takes a couple trips a year on it. I keep telling Joe he is nothing more than a moving target on that thing and it is time to park it. However, he refuses to listen, not that I really expect he would. He will probably continue to ride until somebody has to hold it up for him.

We all know good health is something to really appreciate, especially as we get older. It is also something I enjoy, other than for the fact I have cancer. The doctors all agree my health will stand me in good stead as I move further into treatments. There is also some good longevity into the nineties on my mother's side of the family. So, it is very possible I could have many more years after we kill this cancer, and I think the prospects of that happening are excellent.

It is truly remarkable how many people are praying for us. Every day I get at least one e-mail or card from someone I have never met or heard of. It is both so humbling and encouraging that I can't begin to describe the feeling. It is simply wonderful to know there are so many asking God to heal me. I know He is hearing and answering those prayers from our friends already.

Judy, Leslie, Michael, and I all appreciate your love and concern very much!

Don

****

-----Original Message-----
From: Don Sublett
Sent: Tuesday, May 02, 9:03 AM
To: Support Group
Subject: Update #9

Good Morning, Everyone!

Well, today is radiation treatment day #6. It is also the first day of my second round of chemo—Docetaxel today and Cisplatin tomorrow. I had planned to try not to count days and treatments until I got further into the regimens, but I am only human. Yesterday, I was 1/7 of the way through, and tomorrow, I will be 1/5 completed. What a difference a day makes!

My doctors told me the first couple of weeks would be pretty benign and that seems to be the case, so far. Effects from the treatments are subtle, at this point: the saliva is thickening; tastes are changing slightly; skin on the neck is a little warm/sensitive and showing a slight color change; the tongue is starting to feel like I might have eaten a few too many potato chips; and every-now-and-then the "heartburn express" roars through. Fortunately, the latter doesn't usually hang around very long and I am so glad. This particular heartburn blows through like the "Love Train" in the Coors television commercial. Prilosec will be our "chemical approach" to keep this one in check.

In my research, I learned cancer will touch about one out of every three people. As a powerful reminder, over the weekend I received an e-mail from one of our friends, Tom, who receives these updates. Tom told me his wife, Peggy, is pending a diagnosis of what could well be lung cancer. I know what they are experiencing at the moment and I also know they would most certainly appreciate you remembering them in prayer as they work to get a firm diagnosis and establish an effective course of treatment. Tom and Peggy are the "To" addressees on this message, if you wish to send them a note. The rest of you are "BCC" addressees, in order to keep from giving the world your e-mail address, though I have blown that a couple times already. My apology.

Judy and I continue to receive many cards, letters, phone calls, and e-mails daily, routinely from people we don't know and have never met—friends-of-friends. Friends who will take the time to respond to your friend, whom they don't even know, are very special. Treasure those friends because they will be there for you during your time of need!

Each communication, regardless of form, is encouraging to Judy and me. It is a source of inspiration, both today, and as we move forward. Many of you tell us how encouraging these updates are to you. Some have even used the word "inspiring." If these updates are meaningful to you, then you can only begin to imagine just how much we are inspired by what comes back to us. I sense there are literally hundreds, maybe even thousands of people all over the world praying for God to heal me. I know without a doubt that God is hearing and answering those prayers.

We love and appreciate you so very much!

"Fight's On!!!"

Don

-----Original Message-----
From: Luke Lentz
Sent: Tuesday, May 02, 9:48 AM
To: Don Sublett
Subject: RE: Update #9

Don,

I suspect many others are also keeping your epistles as a testament of your faith. Keep writing as long as it is comfortable. Your witness is encouraging to all of us; and to some who do not fully understand faith, I know they are seeing a light of hope which you so freely give in your writing. We choose each day how we will approach the next twenty-four hours and to always fight and reach for the positives will impact our health, and those around us. No matter the time left for each of us, we *must fight the good fight and not give into doubt, or lose sight of the goal!*

I love you, brother. Yes, you and Judy are in my prayers daily. Been there, done that, and know what you are doing and experiencing with your therapy. Stay the course!

Luke

-----Original Message-----
From: Don Sublett
Sent: Tuesday, May 02, 10:52 AM
To: Luke Lentz
Subject: RE: Update #9

Luke,

Only somebody who has actually been through cancer treatment, as you have, can fully appreciate the impacts of the moment. Sure puts life in a different perspective. I really get encouragement from folks; to be able to provide a little the other direction is a bonus.

Appreciate you and your family!

Don

-----Original Message-----
From: Ralph B.
Sent: Tuesday, May 02, 3:14 PM
To: Don Sublett
Subject: Re: Update #9

Don,

You may not remember me, but I was preaching at Wiesbaden (Germany) when you were in Kaiserslautern and my son Jason was stationed there. I *do* know what you are going thru, since I went thru the same thing about five years ago. All I can tell you to do is exactly what you are doing. Tell everyone you know to pray for you; I believe to this day that is what got me thru the cancer and everything associated with it.

Ralph

-----Original Message-----
From: Don Sublett
Sent: Tuesday, May 02, 4:37 PM
To: Ralph B.
Subject: Re: Update #9

Ralph,

I do remember you. You preached for us a couple times at Kaiserslautern. I also remember your son, Jason, who worshipped with us, as well. Amazing how things just pop into the mind! You are the fourth person I have been in touch with who had this particular cancer. I am glad to hear from another "five-year survivor." As you mention, I will continue to solicit prayers from every corner of the world. I, too, believe prayer to be powerful and effective. I am certain God is setting my mind at ease and working to get me through this.

Thanks for your concern and prayers!

Don

-----Original Message-----
From: John Fuhrmann
Sent: Tuesday, May 02, 6:50 PM
To: Don Sublett
Subject: Re: Update #9

Fight *is* on, Don, and no need to "check six"—you have a ton of friends checking your six with prayers and more prayers, daily. Keep up your match!

Cheers,

John

-----Original Message-----
From: Don Sublett
Sent: Tuesday, May 02, 8:21 PM
To: John Fuhrmann
Subject: Re: Update #9

John,

My spirits are high for a number of reasons:

1) We caught this thing about as early as we could have. We might have chopped a couple of months off if they had sent me for a CT scan immediately, but that just doesn't seem to happen for something of this nature. Apparently, far more (swollen lymph nodes) resolve than not, though, I did tell my Primary Care Manager to put my cancer in the back of her mind next time an old guy like me presents himself with swollen lymph nodes. She concurred.

2) My doctors are superb. I actually have four doctors fully involved in my case. Both of my ENT's, Dr. McMurphy and Dr. Moore, trained at MD Anderson, in Houston. MD Anderson is one of the premier cancer treatment centers in the world and my doctors are up on the latest in treatment, and follow-on surgical requirements. Dr. Moore has both *reputation and respect* among colleagues within the Eglin AFB Hospital as being both a superb and skilled surgeon. Dr. Moore has performed hundreds of radical neck dissections and he told us last week that, of the hundreds he had done following radiation, only two showed residual cancer in the tissues. They are of a mind that, unless there are actual signs of cancer remaining, neck dissection should not be done, and research seems to support that. On the other hand, I think my radiation oncologist is of the mindset, "Why would you not follow the

radiation with neck dissection?" I certainly understand where he is coming from, but I expect my ENT to take charge again when the radiation is completed.

3) My radiation center has the latest in equipment and is using the best techniques known. The techs there are equally sharp. I believe two or three of them are actually physicists.

4) There are hundreds of concerned people praying for us. It is remarkable that people who don't even know us e-mail and tell me they prayed for me today. Makes you believe the best of humanity.

5) God is hearing and answering those prayers. I am certain of that. I am glad you are one of those who are praying for us daily. Thanks, John!

Don

-----Original Message-----
From: Cindy Starnes
Sent: Tuesday, May 02, 5:21 PM
To: Don Sublett
Subject: Re: Update #9

Don & Judy,

We are in Dallas tonight and headed for Amarillo tomorrow, after we visit my Dad in the nursing home.

Thanks for the update. I always feel as if I am reading your diary. Thanks for sharing and becoming so vulnerable to those who love you. I have printed all your reports and have them with us. I re-read them the morning we left Destin and found myself in tears, wishing we had seen you two before we left town. Just know we will be updating our families and they all know about you.

We think of you daily.

Love to you both,

Cindy & Jim

-----Original Message-----
From: Don Sublett
Sent: Tuesday, May 02, 7:43 PM
To: Cindy Starnes
Subject: Re: Update #9

Cindy,

Sharing this experience has been very helpful in my being able to deal with it as I have. People have been very supportive and encouraging of the updates, and in other ways, too. Things are still going well, though some of the effects are a bit less subtle than previous. Still, no pain yet, and that is something to be thankful for. However, that will probably change in the next week or so. Then, we will only have about four weeks of treatments left and *lots* of drugs to rely on!

The guy who goes into radiation right before me has the same cancer and has one week of radiation to go. He is a bit older and had two nodes on the right side surgically removed three weeks prior to starting radiation. He is pretty miserable and was talking today of maybe going into the hospital his last three or four treatment days (for sedation). However, it sounds like he is not being medicated like I expect to be. Time will certainly tell, but things will definitely be changing for us soon.

Enjoy your travels and thanks for staying in touch. Please continue to keep us in your prayers. I know you will. You, too, are in mine.

Don

The gentleman mentioned above was hospitalized and sedated his last week of radiation. He was brought to the clinic each afternoon via ambulance and moved from the stretcher onto the linear accelerator table for his treatment. He created a sense of both fear (at what might be in store for us) and awe (because of how bad he looked), since we each realized that could ultimately be us—very sobering.

****

-----Original Message-----
From: Don Sublett
Sent: Saturday, May 06, 4:31 PM
To: Support Group
Subject: Update #10

Dear Friends,

A couple notes before providing a brief update since my last. Judy is doing well, but is still not back 100%. She was knocked down pretty hard by the pneumonia and it will take a while for her to fully recover. Please continue to pray for her recovery. Also, Tom and Peggy did receive a confirmed diagnosis that Peggy has cancer in her right lung. They will see an oncologist the 11th. I know they will appreciate your continued prayers on their behalf.

Yesterday was day nine of radiation, so we are slightly more than ¼ of the way through the regimen of thirty-five treatment days. I am still feeling well and pain is very minimal. However, swallowing is becoming much more difficult. It is like there is a fist balled up in the back of the throat, so nothing gets down the throat unfelt. Yesterday, it was nearly impossible to swallow, but today it is not so severe. It is easy to see how people lose weight while undergoing treatment for this cancer. You would rather just do without than to disturb the throat by putting anything down it.

As mentioned before, hydration and nutrition are crucial to completing treatment, not to mention the added potential complication of Cisplatin causing kidney failure if hydration is not maintained. We will do what we must and keep in mind there is a feeding tube available. I have to admit, it is tempting to jump right to the feeding tube, but you can only put liquids through it and liquids are not the perfect diet. We will try to maintain as much normalcy as possible until forced to adjust.

Sensing things are starting to heat up a bit, I asked, yesterday, to begin the pain management aspect of the treatment. In response, I was given a pain killer (Lortab) and a mouth elixir nicknamed "Magic Mouth." The latter is a mixture of 1/3 each Benadryl, Maalox, and Xylocaine. Put it in the mouth, swish it around, gargle a bit, and swallow. It numbs anything it touches. I hate to use it for fear of biting the tongue, cheeks, lips, etc., but I can see where it will likely soon become a necessity. Toward the end of treatment, this elixir will probably be replaced with one that is morphine based. If things get that severe and I am not already relying on the feeding tube, I will likely, then, move to it, rather than force anything down the throat.

I am hopeful we can get one more week of treatments in before things start to deteriorate in any significant manner. I can't see where the chemo has impacted me noticeably to this point. However, comments from the doctors and nurses indicate I should start to experience some (perhaps) mild side effects commencing with the next treatments, on Tuesday and Wednesday. At some point, though, I don't know when it will be, the combined effects of the radiation and chemo on the blood will also have an effect. There is no doubt we will have a lot to deal with these remaining five weeks. Please pray there will be no halts in treatment and that I will be able to contend with whatever side effects are presented. I am confident that with your continued support and prayers, God will see us through in as fine a condition as possible.

"Fight's On!!!"

Don

-----Original Message-----
From: Luke Lentz
Sent: Saturday, May 06, 8:36 PM
To: Don Sublett
Subject: RE: Update #10

Don,

I am writing from Minneapolis tonight. Know that you remain in my personal thoughts and prayers. I know things will get tough. Just know there are many who have gone before you and have come out the other side healed and in one piece. I pray for God's gentle hand to hold you and Judy, to comfort you, and to give you the peace that you want.

Love you, brother!

Luke

-----Original Message-----
From: Don Sublett
Sent: Saturday, May 06, 8:14 AM
To: Luke Lentz
Subject: RE: Update #10

Luke,

I appreciate the thoughts and prayers. Prayer is becoming more evident as the key to getting through this. I am a bit surprised that eating has become such a challenge this early on. It is pretty much impossible to get anything down the throat, already. Folks at radiation, the other day, asked if I had put anything down the feeding tube yet and I told them I hadn't had to. Meanwhile, I feel pretty good other than not being able to eat. I expect that will change today, because I can't let my nutrition lag. That is a definite downer, but I will work through it.

There will be a lot of emotions to cope with over the next several weeks. With God's help, we will do fine.

Don

-----Original Message-----
From: Yvonne Borlinghaus
Sent: Wednesday, May 10, 8:49 AM
To: Don Sublett
Subject: Re: Update #10

I don't know how people get through the day without Him, but only by His grace are we able to do so. I remember those days when I thought I could handle it all. I thank Him for touching my heart. I know today will not be an easy day for you, so I have been asking Him to take special care of you today.

Love you.

Yvonne

-----Original Message-----
From: Don Sublett
Sent: Wednesday, May 10, 10:20 AM
To: Yvonne Borlinghaus
Subject: Re: Update #10

Yvonne,

Actually, things are going very well with the treatments. I encountered a *major* roadblock last Friday when I was hit with what I now know was a yeast infection in the mouth. I thought it was the radiation really starting to cook, but it wasn't. It is being treated and I should be able to eat dinner tonight without it killing my throat. Now, I know that is where we are likely headed in another week or two. I didn't think it was supposed to happen that early, and it wasn't.

The request for special care today is being felt here and I greatly appreciate it. Time to hit the shower and grab a bite to eat. Have to head out for chemo at 11:45.

Appreciate the love, concern, and prayers!

Don

****

-----Original Message-----
From: Don Sublett
Sent: Wednesday, May 10, 7:37 PM
To: Support Group
Subject: Update #11

Dear Friends,

I completed the third chemo round of seven and day 12 of 35 radiation sessions, today. I am still feeling very well, but did hit a pretty serious roadblock over the weekend. Recall last Friday when I asked to begin the pain management aspect? Well, as it turns out, that was a bit premature. Prior to Monday's appointment with my Chemo Oncologist, I stopped by the Eglin Dental Clinic to see if I could get in that day, or the next, to get them to take a look at my mouth. Not surprisingly, they took me right back and three dentists came in to examine me. I am an anomaly to them because they don't get many patients with my type cancer and the attendant radiation treatment. Thus, they don't mind building their knowledge and experience base at my expense, and I am perfectly willing to let them. They probably spent 45 minutes with me, just as a walk-in. I can't say enough wonderful things about the staff at the Eglin AFB Hospital!

As it turned out, the cause of the mouth and throat pain is an oral yeast infection. So, I am on Diflucan for five days and then weekly thereafter. (Love those chemists!) The infection is clearing, but I still have a tender mouth. Each day shows improvement. For that, I am very thankful. (As an aside, the nurses at radiation tell me this one is more serious and painful than what women experience. Whether that is true or not, I have new-found appreciation for something which normally affects women more than men. Men, if your wife has a yeast infection, that certainly warrants a breakfast in bed!)

The yeast infection—a side-effect of the radiation—has more than adequately masked any actual pain effects of the radiation on the mouth and the throat. Thus, I think I can safely assume the pain is not very severe at this point. The more noticeable effects of radiation are a thickening and slight reduction in the amount of saliva being produced, and the taste buds continue to change. Judy just baked me a German Chocolate cake. Sure hope it tastes like I remember. Ha!

All things considered, I feel very good at this point. I suspect that will change, but I am hopeful we can get through this week and well into the next before the pain and swelling, which will require pain medication, appear. If that is the case, then we will be approaching the half-way point of treatments! I asked my radiation oncologist, "When will the toxicity start to appear? When can I expect the pain to set in?" His response, "When it happens." I am sure he saw a look in my eyes at his response and he said, "Everybody's different." I wanted to ask, "Don't you have an "average everybody" in there, somewhere?" but I didn't.

One comment: no matter how many doctors and nurses you have, nor how good they are, once you get into a situation like this, you have to *always take the initiative* in making sure your problems are addressed. I mentioned to several at radiation about the pain and swelling in the mouth and throat and asked for the pain meds, but nobody was concerned enough to look in the mouth for something which is common with this type of treatment. They just assumed nine treatments and the burning had set in. Had I not stopped by the Dental Clinic, I don't know when I would have been properly diagnosed.

Things are progressing. I know God is hearing and answering your prayers on my behalf. For that, I am very thankful and ask that those prayers continue for Judy and me. With your prayers and God's help, I know this cancer will die!

"Fight's On!!!"

Don

I don't know if the dentists who examined me were "yanking my chain" or not, but I do not think they were. Evidently they didn't routinely see this condition in an adult, so one of the treatment options they offered was to prescribe *vaginal suppositories* for me to suck on. I experienced mixed emotions when this was offered: glad they had a solution, but not too thrilled to be sucking on vaginal suppositories. Fortunately, Dr. Prieto had a more "modern" solution, which was much preferred.

-----Original Message-----
From: Ellen Smith
Sent: Wednesday, May 10, 9:11 PM
To: Don Sublett
Subject: God loves you!!!!!

Dear Don!

My name is Ellie. I have been praying for you and sending prayer requests all over for you, and others. My husband will soon be gone now for four years. He had cancer, but that is not what took him. Anyway, when he had radiation, he lost all of his saliva, so I started making him chocolate milk shakes with chocolate malt.

After the radiation, we would go home and I would make him one. It really helped him. When he was done with all the radiation and the chemo, it took about three to four months and his saliva glands came back. The doctors feel the chocolate milk shakes and the malt had a big impact on them coming back. I felt I needed to tell you so maybe it could help you, too.

I am a friend of Gerda and Bill (my uncle and his wife). God Bless you and your wife, and may God be with the both of you, always. Without Jesus, where would we all be?

I am not a good speller, so I hope you understand what I have written.

Ellie

-----Original Message-----
From: Don Sublett
Sent: Wednesday, May 10, 10:19 PM
To: Ellen Smith
Subject: God loves you!!!!!

Ellie,

I understood very clearly what you wrote. Thank you for sharing that with me. Right now, I am having a hard time tolerating the cold, because of the tenderness from the yeast infection. However, I am a milk shake lover and I hope I can soon, once again, be able to tolerate cold in the mouth. When that happens...!

Judy and I appreciate prayers on our behalf. We know, without a doubt, God is hearing and answering them every day. Without Jesus, we would all be lost, and that would be a terrible thing to contemplate. Fortunately, we don't have to worry!

Thanks again for your concern and prayers.

Don

-----Original Message-----
From: Dan Scott
Sent: Thursday, May 11, 6:08 PM
To: Don Sublett
Subject: Re: Update #11

Brother Don,

Your e-mails are a great encouragement to me. You should write the great American novel some day. The fight may be on, but you are already a winner and leading other folks to stay the course. You and Judy are in my heart, mind, and prayers. Good job!

Dan

-----Original Message-----
From: Don Sublett
Sent: Thursday, May 11, 9:35 PM
To: Dan Scott
Subject: Re: Update #11

Dan,

I appreciate the kind words of encouragement, but these updates will likely be the closest I ever get to that novel.

We love and appreciate you. I know God does, as well!

Don

-----Original Message-----
From: Brad Bynum
Sent: Friday, May 12, 8:31 AM
To: Don Sublett
Subject: Re: Update #11

Don,

Thanks for the update. Your gratitude and faith is infectious! Your good comment about taking the initiative regarding your own treatment is a great lesson, as well. I sense no bitterness, no victim mentality, but speaking the truth in love until some real satisfaction/relief was found. I love your faith and perseverance. It reminds me of when Nehemiah and his men "prayed to our God and posted a guard..." and neither I, nor my brothers, nor my men, nor the guards with me took off our clothes; each had his weapon, even when he went for water." (Nehemiah 4:9 & 23) That is how Nehemiah said, "Our God will fight for us!" (Nehemiah 4:20)

Faithful prayer with personal vigilance is right and righteous. Fight on, my brother!

Love,

Brad

-----Original Message-----
From: Don Sublett
Sent: Friday, May 12, 1:13 PM
To: Brad Bynum
Subject: Re: Update #11

Brad,

Thanks for the encouraging note. You did correctly sense my attitude—no bitterness, etc.

People get busy and just don't always have time to "fine tune" their efforts. Thus, you need to continue to look out for yourself. I am convinced God is hearing and answering prayer on our behalf. We continue to march along in pretty good condition and we are almost through three of the seven weeks of treatment. If we can get one more in before things start to go noticeably south, I would be one grateful puppy!

Sure appreciate having dedicated prayer warriors like you and Lori taking my needs before God!

Love you, Brother!

Don

-----Original Message-----
From: Laurie Willcox
Sent: Sunday, May 14, 6:24 PM
To: Don Sublett
Subject: Re: Update #11

Mr. Sublett,

Thanks for keeping us in the loop with your progress. I am glad to hear things are going well. I hope that continues and I pray the next week or so continues to give you some comfort, instead of pain. You are a fighter and that is what matters the most. There is something comforting about seeing doctors and going through horrible treatments. Strange, I know, but true. At least that was/is the case for me. Keep up the good fight!

Love,

Laurie

-----Original Message-----
From: Don Sublett
Sent: Sunday, May 14, 9:49 PM
To: Laurie Willcox
Subject: Re: Update #11

Laurie,

I am still feeling well, but this yeast infection in my mouth is about the worst thing imaginable. I presume it is getting better, but everything I put in my mouth tastes like a glob of salt. Horrible! Add to that, all of the food commercials on TV and...ha! One of the best moves I ever made in my life was to have the feeding tube inserted. It has been a genuine blessing. It is about impossible to put anything solid in the mouth, so I might have starved to death, already, without it.

I will see a doctor or two tomorrow, so I am hoping one will give me something which will go ahead and rid me of the rest of the yeast problem. Other than that, pain is minimal and largely due to the mouth sores from the yeast. I expect that will begin to change, but I know God is answering prayer, so it doesn't have to.

Tomorrow will be the end of week three, so there are four more treatment weeks to go. Would love to "breeze" through another week or two, but don't know how that will track. I certainly pray we don't have to halt treatments because of the effects of the radiation on the blood. I am confident we will get the yeast under control, but I expect there will likely be something else to deal with as it clears. That just seems to be the nature of the beast. Chemo has yet to prove to be a problem, but that, too, is cumulative. So, I don't know if there will be problems from it or not. It is an adjunct to the radiation, so it is possible the overall effects will be negligible. One can hope, huh?

There are no nerve endings at the base of the tongue, but there are plenty elsewhere, which are being hit by the radiation. Everyone says I will start to feel things soon, but I am not going to worry about it. When it happens, I am sure I will realize it. I have a good team of doctors and they are doing everything imaginable to get me through this with the least amount of discomfort. Ultimately, God is in control, so we know we are in good hands, huh?

Love you guys!

Don

****

-----Original Message-----
From: Don Sublett
Sent: Monday, May 15, 9:33 PM
To: Support Group
Subject: Update #12

Good Evening, All:

Well, today wrapped up the third week of radiation treatments—twenty remain, along with four weeks of chemo. These last four weeks are likely going to be something to behold, but that will come as no surprise. I have been briefed and prepped more than once by everyone involved.

Today was an eventful day and I am very pleased we are approaching the half-way point, as things are definitely beginning to "heat up" in the mouth and throat areas. I met with my radiation oncologist, Dr. Bonanno, today, both before and after the treatment. He made some changes to my treatment plan in order to salvage as much of the saliva glands as possible. Thus, I spent an extra 20 minutes or so immobilized on the treatment table as they re-measured to adjust/modify some of the angles and settings. From the rectangles I still have drawn on my neck, it looks like they are going to be able to cut a pretty wide swath around them. If this works, it will potentially alleviate or reduce "dry mouth," which is one of the most annoying after-effects of the treatment.

The yeast infection in the mouth has continued to cause consternation. Food swells up to what seems about three times its normal size and almost refuses to go down. Thus, I have taken few solids by mouth over the last week, but I have continued to take in fluids orally. Also, everything tastes like a big old glob of burned salt - horrible! That is probably due to the taste buds going. Thank goodness Dr. Prieto emphasized the feeding tube! It has been—and will be—a *major* asset these weeks. I don't want it to be too much of a crutch, because the throat and neck muscles still need to be exercised.

There is another guy at radiation, a few slots behind me, who has the same cancer. He is also, probably, a couple weeks behind me in treatment. I spoke briefly with him today and learned he has no feeding tube. He is pretty cavalier in his attitude about needing to lose weight. I think he is likely, soon, to be in for a major reality check. Last Friday, the guy right before me finished his radiation treatments for the same cancer. At his request, he was hospitalized and sedated his last four days of treatment. He, too, had a feeding tube. He'd had treatments halted for a period and was getting a double dose of radiation twice daily for his last couple weeks of care. So, his case was a bit extreme and also why

I pray we don't have to halt treatments for any reason. So far, my lab work is "excellent." Please pray it continues to be so.

Dr. Bonanno also did his usual exam of the neck area and commented that the cancerous lymph node on each side of the neck is shrinking. So, it is obvious the treatments are working in those areas. It is also becoming more apparent that the treatment is having impact in the back of the throat and on the cancer, in the base of the tongue. Last Friday, swallowing was still fairly easy. As the weekend wore on, swallowing got progressively more difficult. This evening, it is becoming readily apparent that the tissue in the throat area is really starting to cook. I have avoided the pain meds to this point, because there has really been no pain. However, Dr. Bonanno suggested today that I begin taking the Lortab. I hate to start down that path, but I think he is correct in telling me to do so.

All things considered, I am still doing very well. I am hopeful we can get this week behind us before having to go on the morphine patch. However, as soon as I detect the Lortab is not doing its job, I will not hesitate to ask to be bumped up to the next level. I am not proud.

We do appreciate *very much* the cards, letters, phone calls, visits, e-mails and most especially, your *prayers!* I have every confidence God is hearing and answering those prayers, and that is why we are as far into this as we are with minimal problems. There is no doubt things are changing pretty rapidly now, but I am confident God is going to be with us every step of the way. In fact, there will probably be times like in the poem, "Footprints," where there will only be one set of footprints in the sand. That is when, because of your prayers, He will be carrying me through this. There is no better place to be!

"Fight's On!!!"

Don

-----Original Message-----
From: Yvonne Borlinghaus
Sent: Monday, May 15, 9:14 PM
To: Don Sublett
Subject: Re: Update #12

You are a champion and my hero. Thank you for giving us the information to share your journey. It does help us to know how you are doing. Many prayers are going up daily from our end. We care so much and don't question why bad things happen to good people. That is a new step for me. I am with you about Him carrying us, because there are some things we just can't do on our own. Thank God for the pain medication. It is there to make things bearable. Hope you have a restful night. You've got Carol there this week to keep you in line.

Love you,

Yvonne

-----Original Message-----
From: Don Sublett
Sent: Monday, May 15, 10:24 PM
To: Yvonne Borlinghaus
Subject: Re: Update #12

Yvonne,

I am very fortunate to have a lot of friends and family who are tuned in to what is going on, and are begging to help out. We really appreciate the prayers and your willingness to come over and lend a hand. Not everyone is so fortunate.

I have never questioned why this has happened to me. Stuff just happens. I made my bed somewhere along the way and I am now having to deal with it. I think it is the Apostle James that tells us God is responsible for the good things. There will be a lot of good to come out of this. I am certain of that.

Carol and Judy are really enjoying themselves this week. It is good for them to be together. Of course, for me, too!

We love you all!

Don

-----Original Message-----
From: Lee G.
Sent: Monday, May 15, 9:27 PM
To: Don Sublett
Subject: RE: Update #12

Don,

You are one tough old bird. Not sure I would be able to give a blow-by-blow account. Glad to hear the lymph nodes are shrinking and that the docs think they can salvage some of the salivary glands. Sounds like the battle is in your favor.

As always, we will keep praying and you just keep on fighting. If I may ask, how is Judy doing and holding up?

Lee

-----Original Message-----
From: Don Sublett
Sent: Monday, May 15, 9:43 PM
To: Lee G.
Subject: RE: Update #12

Lee,

I hope I am as tough as I need to be. Morphine will provide "courage." The doctors are doing everything they can to kill the cancer and then leave me in the best position possible for recovery. I am very fortunate to have the medical care available to me that I do. The bill for the first two weeks totaled over $27,000. Tri-Care will not pay all of that, but these people do take Tri-Care. My share is $12.00 per visit.

Judy is doing well. So far, I am able to take care of myself. I may have to give over partial care sometime in the next couple weeks, but I should never be fully out of the picture. So, she is holding up well. Starting this week, we will have another family member here to give us support and a hand when needed. All things considered, this is about as optimum as we could make it. We are very fortunate to have people to lean on.

We do appreciate the prayers very much. Without them, I would probably be a basket case. As you say, we will continue to fight and pray. God will get us through this.

Appreciate you!

Don

-----Original Message-----
From: G. Millon Plyler
Sent: Monday, May 15, 9:50 PM
To: Don Sublett
Subject: RE: Update #12

Thanks for your update. It is touching, but also a reality check of what you are going through. I prayed for you while on my walk tonight. I hope God doesn't mind me asking help for "my list" of people over and over, because I have got friends, people I don't know, etc., and I keep "going to the well" with them to the Lord, over and over. I *know* He hears and helps. I will get you on "my list" again in a few minutes, as I am heading to bed. Take care, and may God bless you and your family. Keep up the fight!

Millon

-----Original Message-----
From: Don Sublett
Sent: Monday, May 15, 9:55 PM
To: G. Millon Plyler
Subject: RE: Update #12

Millon,

I know God doesn't mind one bit. I really appreciate you.

Don

-----Original Message-----
From: Wanda Nobles
Sent: Monday, May 15, 10:14 PM
To: Don Sublett
Subject: Re: Update #12

Hey!

Almost halfway there! Keep your chin up, Buddy! This will soon be a memory you can file away and then get on with your life! It will be something you will look back on and see how God did His great work in you! It is only in our greatest weakness that we are able to see His greatest strength!

I love you and never stop praying for you in the wee hours, when I wake up. You and Judy are always in my heart. I think of you and pray for you when I am on my long walks in the woods, or on the beach. There is always a song coming to mind which makes me think of you and what you are going through. I never know what to do to help, but if prayers, thoughts, and wishes can help, then you are golden!

Love you so much! Call if you need me. I am still here if you need someone to yell at!

Wanda

-----Original Message-----
From: Don Sublett
Sent: Monday, May 16, 7:55 AM
To: Wanda Nobles
Subject: Re: Update #12

Wanda,

We really appreciate you and your constant thoughts of us. God *is* hearing those prayers and answering them each day.

I think these narcotics are going to take the edge off of my needing to yell at anyone and you'd be the last one on that particular list anyway.

We love you!

Don

-----Original Message-----
From: Lori Bynum
Sent: Tuesday, May 16, 4:43 AM
To: Don Sublett
Subject: Re: Update #12

Dear Don,

Brad and I are praying for you. I know God is surrounding you with his angels to help you get through this challenging time. I know He is helping you physically and emotionally. I think of the scripture in Isaiah 49:15-16 "Can a mother forget the baby at her breast and have no compassion on the child she has borne? Though she may forget, *I will not forget you!* See, I have engraved you on the palms of my hands."
God Bless you and Judy.

We love you,

Lori

-----Original Message-----
From: Don Sublett
Sent: Tuesday, May 16, 8:40 AM
To: Lori Bynum
Subject: Re: Update #12

Lori,

I think you know the truth of the matter very well. Judy and I appreciate the love and prayers so very much.

We love you, too!

Don

-----Original Message-----
From: Curt Seebaldt
Sent: Tuesday, May 16, 8:31 AM
To: Don Sublett
Subject: RE: Update #12

Don,

No time to get depressed. Just think about the eight or ten year-old with cancer (now that is depressing!). The pain meds are there for a reason and you should not hesitate to take them. That only indicates you are into the tough stages of treatment and need some help getting through it. Just let me know if I need to take you to the treatment center. I should not be going anywhere soon.

Cobalt

-----Original Message-----
From: Don Sublett
To: Curt Seebaldt
Sent: Tuesday, May 16, 6:08 PM
Subject: RE: Update #12

Curt,

The pain meds are effective and I plan to use them to the extent necessary. Enduring constant pain could certainly lead to depression. As I get closer to the end, the pain meds will make the pain tolerable, but will not totally kill it, unless I am different than the others I have talked to about it. This is just a fork in the road, but a necessary one.

I really appreciate the offer of transportation. We will have other family members here through the end of treatment and well into recovery, so I will be using them. We are fortunate that several on Judy's side have offered to come spend a week or two with us, as well as my sister, and Les and Michael. Still, your offer means a lot to me.

Don

-----Original Message-----
From: Lynn G.
Sent: Tuesday, May 16, 1:41 PM
To: Don Sublett
Subject: Re: Update #12

Don,

Just wanted to touch base and let you know you continue to be in our thoughts and prayers, as well as in our church family's prayers, here in Tallahassee. We continue to count down the days/weeks with you! So glad to hear you are doing as well as you are, this far into the treatments. Just goes to show you God truly does hear and answer prayers, and we are so glad for that!

How's the grass?

Much Love,

Lynn and Travis

-----Original Message-----
From: Don Sublett
Sent: Tuesday, May 16, 6:26 PM
To: Lynn G.
Subject: Re: Update #12

Lynn/Travis,

Good to hear from you. We continue to appreciate and experience the blessings of God. I know He's responsible for things going as well as they are. We really are blessed in so many ways, though sometimes that might not be so easy to see or feel. I hope to not lose sight of that as we move forward. Please pray that I do not.

We love you guys!

Don

P.S.: The grass is under control and Judy is thrilled. I couldn't care less. Ha!

-----Original Message-----
From: Fred Peery
Sent: Friday, May 19, 8:28 PM
To: Don Sublett
Subject: Re: Update #12

Don,

We read your reports and all we can feel is your bravery, your patience, and your faith. We feel God is holding your hand through this ordeal and want you to know our prayers and our admiration are constant.

In Christian love,

Lucy and Fred

-----Original Message-----
From: Don Sublett
Sent: Friday, May 19, 8:31 PM
To: Fred P.
Subject: Re: Update #12

Lucy and Fred,

Thank you for the kind words of encouragement. They mean a lot to me, as do your prayers and thoughtfulness.

In Christ,

Don

-----Original Message-----
From: Larry Lewis
Sent: Saturday, May 20, 8:33 PM
To: Don Sublett
Subject: Re: Update #12

I know it is much more difficult than you are stating, but I am glad it is going well and bearable. Best to you and Judy. Hope she is feeling better. We will be fishing again before you know it, so keep on truckin'.

Larry

-----Original Message-----
From: Don Sublett
Sent: Saturday, May 20, 8:33 PM
To: Larry Lewis
Subject: Re: Update #12

Larry,

Good to hear from you! Actually, things are going very well and have been easier than what I was told to expect. This has been a pretty good week. The mouth situation is starting to come under control, though I am not sure it will be "right" again until after the treatment is over and I have begun to recover. That is probably the most disappointing thing encountered, so far. All the literature said there would be problems in the mouth and throat, but I don't think I appreciated just how severe they might be. Just not being able to eat affects you psychologically, but I am using the heck out of the feeding tube in order to keep the nutrition and hydration up. I lost over 13 pounds as of earlier this week and my ENT doc gave me a lot of grief, so I have gained some of the pounds back and now am down only about ten. I would easily be down 20-30 pounds if I didn't have the feeding tube.

Pain is minimal, or the Lortab is just doing a good job covering it. At some point, they will really start to burn the tongue to kill the cancer and that is when the real difficult period will set in. Though there are no nerve endings in the base of the tongue, I expect the areas around it to feel/show the effects. That will probably start to occur over the next five or six radiation treatments. I have 17 radiation treatments left and the doctors tell me the last two weeks will be very hard. If the tough period is just the last two weeks of treatment and the two or three weeks to follow, then I am far better off than what I have been told I'd be, or imagined all along. That is not to minimize things, because I am not looking forward to going through it, but will be glad to have it behind me.

I know there are a lot of people praying for me and I am dead certain God is hearing and answering those prayers. For that I am *very* thankful.

Don

P.S.: Judy is doing well and said to tell you, "Hi!"

****

-----Original Message-----
From: Don Sublett
Sent: Monday, May 22, 1:10 PM
To: Dr. McMurphy
Subject: Tongue Ulcers

Dr. McMurphy,

Don't know if you have anything else in your arsenal or not, but we are losing the battle with the tongue ulcers from the radiation. I am on 100mg of Diflucan, 800mg Zovirax, and swishing and swallowing the Carafate. In addition, I am gargling four or five times a day with salt water and baking soda.

I went to the Dental Clinic this morning and the two doctors who examined me said tissue is dying in the mouth from the chemo and radiation, which we knew. Neither had anything else to offer. I sense, though I may be wrong, they are somewhat hesitant to prescribe anything for fear of upsetting things further. I have an appointment with Dr. Prieto this afternoon, prior to radiation, and will query him as well.

All-in-all, I am doing very well at this point, but would like to try and reign in the mouth problems as much as possible.

Thank you!

Don Sublett

-----Original Message-----
From: Dr. McMurphy
Sent: Monday, May 22, 4:10 PM
To: Don Sublett
Subject: RE: Tongue Ulcers

Mr. Sublett,

Keep up what you are doing. Unfortunately, we know that the mouth could get even worse. I will do some more research. What is the count-down at today? The end is in sight!

Dr. Mac

-----Original Message-----
From: Don Sublett
Sent: Monday, May 22, 9:12 PM
To: Dr. McMurphy
Subject: RE: Tongue Ulcers

Dr. Mac,

Appreciate the response. I have completed 18 of 35 treatments, but Dr. Bonnano halted my treatment before today's (Monday) session because of the weight loss in the face and neck. F.Y.I., I am down 10.5 pounds from what I weighed when treatments began. It is very obvious in the face and neck areas. They made a new mask, did a new CT scan today, and are building a new radi-ation plan.

Dr. Bonnano didn't tell me when he thinks we will resume, but indicated it probably will not be this week. I am guessing it might be next Monday before we pick up again. This halt might let the mouth heal some, but I suspect as "burned" as it is, that it probably will not recover a whole lot.

Some of the literature I was given mentions a product called, Gelclair[3]. It seems to have been developed for my condition. I mentioned it to the dentists today, but they have never heard of Gelclair. I am willing to try it if you are willing to write it. I doubt the base carries it. Also, Dr. Prieto mentioned he thinks I am experiencing about the max pain I will feel. I mentioned that to Dr. B and he seemed to think it would still intensify some, but probably not a whole lot more. I am feeling pretty "comfortable" at the moment. So, I must admit, I am somewhat skeptical of their assessment, since there is a lot of burning/killing left in 17 treatments. I am still on Lortab and I will be very (pleasantly) surprised if they are correct.

I will call Dr. Prieto tomorrow and let him know radiation is halted. He doesn't want to do any chemo if I am not getting radiation.

I sure appreciate your care and concern, and hope I am not being too much of a pest.

Very Kindly,

Don

****

-----Original Message-----
From: Don Sublett
Sent: Monday, May 22, 8:00 PM
To: Support Group
Subject: Update #13

Good Evening Friends,

Monday is always an interesting day, since I usually meet with my two oncologists. Today was no exception. I was informed at radiation, today, that radiation treatment is being halted, probably for the remainder of the week, so my radiation treatment plan can be completely redesigned. I figured if this happened it would be due to complications in the blood caused by the radiation, but this is not the case. The reason for the halt is weight loss. I have lost ten pounds, which isn't a lot, since most I have talked to lost 25 pounds or more since starting treatments; however, the loss really shows in the face and neck. There is now a lot of "space" under my mask. Or, there was, since they made me a new mask this afternoon and did another CT scan on which to base the new treatment plan.

As mentioned previously, the treatment plan is designed to be extremely precise. The density of the tissue, how far the radiation needs to penetrate, distances between the body and the machine and many other factors all play into the physics equations which guide the treatment. The doctor is concerned that they know exactly how much radiation is being directed to each area and considers the weight loss as throwing their treatment plan off. It will most likely be early next week before I get back on the table and resume the last 17 radiation treatments. I really hate that there is a halt, but the doctor didn't seem to think we will lose much of the ground gained.

The upside of the halt is that it may give the mouth a slight chance to heal. The yeast infection really did a number on me before we got it under control. There have been some sores to develop on the sides of the tongue, as a result. These probably stand little to no chance of healing while being bombarded with protons and electrons, but now may have a very slight chance. With the changes to the mouth caused by the radiation, it is doubtful a week will be enough time, but one can hope and pray for some healing in the interim.

I am almost hesitant to mention the following for fear of being perceived like the little boy who cried, "Wolf!" but I must. Of particular interest, today, was a comment from Dr. Prieto (chemo). He thinks I am near the max in the amount of pain I will experience. He said that near the mid-point of treatments, effects generally are near their peak. I mentioned this to Dr. Bonanno (radiation) and he seemed a bit surprised. Dr. Bonnano felt the pain level would still increase some. However, neither seemed to believe it would be as intense as what I had been told to expect. Both seemed to follow the same reasoning: good hydration (key); good nutrition (key); good health (key); somewhat early detection of the tumor; tumor location; attitude; age; general health; following instructions; etc.

You are very aware of what the doctors prepared me for and I am still not sure either of them is right, or even close, in their assessment of how much the pain will increase. I have described some of the patients I have seen with the same cancer and also mentioned Walt and Sanford. All experienced extreme levels of pain. Each also wound up on the morphine patch. Still, there is no denying the pain I am experiencing at the moment is being addressed very well by the Lortab and I am at the mid-point of treatment. I sit here this evening very "comfortable."

The factors the doctors mentioned are certainly relevant, but there is one thing which is for certain: There is absolutely no denying the fact God's hand is actively involved, because of the many prayers offered in our behalf! I don't know what will unfold in the next three weeks, or so, health or pain-wise, once treatments resume, but I do know God will continue to hear and answer your prayers. Judy and I are blessed to have such wonderfully supportive and prayerful friends.

Please continue those prayers, with full knowledge that God is answering them daily!

"Fight's On!!!"

Don

-----Original Message-----
From: G. Millon Plyler
Sent: Monday, May 22, 8:28 PM
To: Don Sublett
Subject: RE: Update #13

I have specifically asked the Lord to ease your pain, as well as destroy your cancer. I know HE answers prayers. I will continue praying and you keep fighting. Take care.

Millon

-----Original Message-----
From: Don Sublett
Sent: Monday, May 22, 9:18 PM
To: G. Millon Plyler
Subject: RE: Update #13

Millon,

Sleep well tonight knowing God is answering those prayers. I am sleeping like a baby.

Don

-----Original Message-----
From: Mike Bagwell
Sent: Monday, May 22, 8:46 PM
To: Don Sublett
Subject: RE: Update #13

Don,

I think it is great news! You haven't lost much weight, less than what I thought you would have, by now. The yeast infection also sounds much better now. Problems with the mouth ulcers, I understand, because I get them occasionally. Although, I am sure much less severe; but it sounds like they might be healing, as well, in the coming days—at least somewhat, if not completely. Will the chemo continue, or is it on hold, as well?

Regarding the pain, everyone perceives pain differently. You may have just a stronger tolerance for pain. Penny says it is a good thing I was never captured and interrogated under torture, because I would have given up everything so fast they would have thought I was lying, and then *really* started torturing me. LOL! But seriously, not experiencing as much pain as you thought you would have is definitely good, even if it does continue to get worse.

How is Judy doing? Is there anything we can do?

Our prayers continue for you both, and for your friend. How is she doing? Did she start treatments yet?

Prayerfully,

Mike

-----Original Message-----
From: Don Sublett
Sent: Monday, May 22, 9:28 PM
To: Mike Bagwell
Subject: RE: Update #13

Mike,

I was surprised at the halt in treatment, since, like you say, ten pounds is not a lot to lose. Still, being where it is showing, I guess it is significant.

These mouth ulcers are pretty good size, but the Lortab is killing that pain, too. I am not putting solids in the mouth (trying to not irritate the tongue) but continue to drink and swallow, take my pills, etc. I don't know how strong a pain killer the Lortab is, but it is being effective to this point. Pain bumps up a little when it starts to wear off, but it is at a tolerable level. I fully expect the pain to increase some, because they painted a pretty grim pain picture for me when I started. Things haven't come close to what I had been told to expect, but I am sure God has a big hand in that, too.

Our friend, Peggy, still has not begun treatment, but I'd expect her to begin in the next couple of weeks.

We are all doing fine and don't need any help with anything at the moment, but I certainly appreciate you asking and offering to help. We will have another family member here with us, though I am now wondering if it is really necessary, through mid-July—just in case things get too tough for Judy to handle alone. Please know we do appreciate the prayers, and also know they are absolutely being heard and answered. God is taking good care of me.

Love you guys!

Don

-----Original Message-----
From: Wanda Nobles
Sent: Monday, May 22, 8:46 PM
To: Don Sublett
Subject: Re: Update #13

Dearest Don,

I sit here with tears in my eyes as I read your update and I think they are tears of gratitude to the Father for answering all the prayers sent up that you would be as comfortable as possible through this ordeal. As I have told you before, I can't stand the thought of you being in extreme pain and would take it myself, if it would help you. It gives me joy beyond measure to know you are sitting at home in a reasonable amount of comfort! I am sorry about the treatments being halted, in that it just makes it last longer, but it may be the Father's way of giving you the time you need to heal a little more. He always knows what you need more than we, or the doctors, do.

I really miss seeing your lovable mug, but am so afraid of bringing germs and sickness to you. We have had one bug after another going through our home, with the kids and grandkids. Right now, I am feeling fine and dandy. My throat is not hurting at all anymore, but the girls have had some kind of strange virus that gives them bumps on their tongues and affects their taste buds. I am sure it is all connected somehow and I certainly don't want to be responsible for bringing you any more to deal with than you already have! Please forgive me for not being there.

It was great meeting your sister Sunday morning! We had a great deal of fun in Bible class, with both your sister and Judy's sister there to egg us on to even more mischief than usual—if that is possible! They both said Judy and I make a great team, and I would have to agree, even

114

though we do bring out the "rotten" side in each other! Of course, I guess that is why we enjoy each other's company so much!

Sorry for going on so long; just lonesome, I guess! Take care, sweet friend. Get a lot of rest and relaxation this week, and be ready to fight the rest of the fight with even more vigor and confidence than ever before! I have all the faith and confidence in the world in both the Father, and in you, His vessel!

Love you much!

Wanda

-----Original Message-----
From: Don Sublett
Sent: Monday, May 22, 10:35 PM
To: Wanda Nobles
Subject: Re: Update #13

Wanda,

You are a real treasure. I hope you tell Mike that often!

I find myself humbled at the grace and love God is showing me as my treatment proceeds. He is truly taking care of me in so many ways and I find myself thanking him very often for watching over me. I can't imagine how folks without Him in their lives manage to get through something like this, but they do. I suppose that is just testimony to how strong the human spirit can be. Pair the human spirit with the Holy Spirit, faith in God, the strength drawn from Christ, and life is so much better.

I do miss getting out; particularly to church, but know it is more prudent for me to guard my health at the moment. I will be glad when things return to "normal" and getting together will again just be something we do, though I am not sure what normal will be from now on. I know I have been changed by this experience and probably don't yet know all the ways that will be borne out of it. I do know I will certainly be more open in sharing my faith and what God has done for me. Boy, do I have a story to tell!

I hate you have these bugs that keep bouncing around in the family, but I do appreciate your consciousness about not "sharing" them with me. Everyone has been real good in their consideration of me and my sensitive immune system. Judy and I are fortunate to have good family support. My sister and I have not been particularly close, but this is giving us a chance to draw closer, and that is good. She has lost two husbands, one to a heart attack, and the other to cancer. She is certainly in a position to be able to lend support. I will take advantage of the opportunity to get some rest and try to heal in the mouth, but I do look forward to treatments starting back up so we can finish the job of killing this cancer.

We love you all!

Don

-----Original Message-----
From: Dr. McMurphy
Sent: Tuesday, May 23, 7:11 AM
To: Don Sublett
Subject: RE: Tongue Ulcers

Mr. Sublett,

I am willing to write whatever necessary to try and help with the mucositis. Gelclair is not on the pharmacy formulary. Research and let me know how and where to prescribe it for you. 10.5 lbs is great. That means you gained four since I last saw you! Just talked to Dr. Bonnano. He said this is fairly routine and your scan looked good. We will plan your CT/PET for six weeks after completion of treatment. Keep your spirits up. (You are not a pest!)

Dr. Mac

-----Original Message-----
From: Don Sublett
Sent: Tuesday, May 23, 8:25 AM
To: Dr. McMurphy
Subject: RE: Tongue Ulcers

Dr. Mac,

If you will write a script, I will take it to Walgreen's and get it filled today. This link shows how the prescription should be written: http://www.gelclair.com/. Will probably need some refills.

From the website info, it looks like most pharmacies will not stock the Gelclair, but can have it within 24-hours. I will stop out around 11:00 and pick it up, if that is ok.

Thanks so much,

Don

-----Original Message-----
From: Bernie Hendricks
Sent: Tuesday, May 23, 9:30 AM
To: Don Sublett
Subject: RE: Update #13

Thanks for the update, Don. I feel like I am right there with you and experiencing it myself.

God keep you.

B. H.

-----Original Message-----
From: Don Sublett
Sent: Tuesday, May 23, 1:39 PM
To: Bernie Hendricks
Subject: RE: Update #13

Bernie,

I get a lot of favorable comments about the updates. I am glad to provide them and think they help encourage people to keep praying for me. There is no doubt God is hearing and answering those prayers. I was just out to see my ENT about a prescription for the tongue ulcers and she once again emphasized how good and healthy I am looking. I think she, too, is surprised.

Sure appreciate the prayers,

Don

-----Original Message-----
From: Sanford Flach
Sent: Tuesday, May 23, 4:37 PM
To: Don Sublett
Subject: Re: I received the update

Hi Don,

Glad you are doing so well!

We hope you continue to tolerate your treatments as well as you have so far. Have you had to use your feeding tube yet? Do you have to use the liquid pain killer for your throat before you eat?

Sanford

-----Original Message-----
From: Don Sublett
Sent: Tuesday, May 23, 7:39 PM
To: Sanford Flach
Subject: Re: I received the update

Sanford,

Because of the mouth problems (ulcers), I am using the feeding tube for pretty much all of my nutrition. That will probably continue until I'm done. I have a huge ulcer on the right side of my tongue and eating food irritates it. I am trying to minimize the damage to the extent that I can. Everything tastes burnt and horrible. The salty taste isn't as bad as it was, but it still lingers a bit. I am able to drink fluids (mainly water) and do so, because I know I need to use the throat muscles to the extent possible. I'm also still taking my pills by mouth. A couple of them are fairly good size, so the throat is still pretty open.

F.Y.I., I am taking Ensure Plus and beefing it up with a protein powder the nutritionist recommended. I mix that with milk and add some honey once or twice a day. After finished, one of them will have between 700 and 800 calories. I am trying to do at least three of them a day in order to hit 86 grams of protein and 2,000 calories. I am also drinking some Gatorade and Propel water to keep the electrolytes and vitamins and minerals up, too. My doctors all know my approach to nutrition and none have any objections. Their concern is that I keep my weight up and stay hydrated. The feeding tube has been my salvation to this point. I would easily be down 30-40 pounds if I didn't have it.

I was given some Magic Mouth the second weekend I was in radiation. I have used it, but since I am not taking many solids, I haven't used it for a while. I hate the numb feeling that it provides, but imagine at some point numbness might be a beautiful thing.

Quite honestly, Sanford, everyone is amazed I am doing so well at this point. I almost feel like, if I include myself in the "everyone," I am denying I thought God would answer the many prayers being offered. I suppose it is ok to be amazed at the goodness of God, at times. I know He is certainly blessing me right now!

Because of the scenario my doctors gave me, conversations with you, Walt, and people I have seen at radiation with the same cancer, I kept wondering, "When is the shoe going to fall?" Now, they are trying to lead me to believe that it may not. I am hopeful the doctors are right, but I refuse to let myself buy into the new scenario completely. I have 17 radiation treatments left and know there is still a lot of burning and killing to come. Thus, there is still plenty of time for things to get ugly. Yet, I know God is deeply involved and continues to answer prayer daily in my life.

I don't know how the remaining three weeks of treatment will play out once I get started again. However, I am very hopeful, at this point, I will get through the treatment with less trauma than I anticipated. I attribute that to good doctors, good medicine, being the best patient I can, and to God's healing hand. People have been wonderfully supportive of us and I am so humbled at the love and concern being shown.

We serve a wonderful God!

Don

****

-----Original Message-----
From: Don Sublett
Sent: Friday, May 26, 10:56 PM
To: Support Group
Subject: Update #14

Good Evening Friends,

I went to the radiation oncologist this afternoon for the "dry run," prior to resuming both radiation and chemo next Tuesday. They put me on the table and spent close to two hours getting the alignment right and making tweaks to the new treatment plan. The doc says we didn't lose much ground by having eleven days off, but I can still feel the lymph nodes on both sides of the neck. Both have shrunk dramatically but are still not dead. I can't say if they have grown this last week or not, but I suspect they probably have. There remains a lot of killing to be done these last 17 treatments.

The yeast problem in the mouth is under control and the tongue/mouth sores are showing signs of healing. A couple days ago I was given a medication (Gelclair), which is fairly new to the market. It was developed specifically for radiation and chemo patients, but is also usable for "normal" mouth problems. After using only four packets, I can see improvement. My appreciation for chemists continues to grow.

My throat is still in good condition, but I continue to use the feeding tube for my nutrition. One reason is, anything other than water irritates the tongue sores. Continually irritating the sores will hinder healing. Also, food still has very poor taste, but certainly not as bad as last week. In fact, I went to the Dairy Queen Wednesday and got a banana milk shake to try. I drank part of it, but the tongue was getting irritated, so I had to toss it. I think it is just about impossible to find anything which doesn't have salt in it.

A couple updates ago I mentioned the guy with, what I felt, was a pretty cavalier attitude. I saw him today and he said things are starting to get rough. He is experiencing the same mouth problems I am and pain is becoming a problem. (He is now on two pain medications: Lortab and Fentanyl.) I told him to insist his doctor prescribe Gelclair before he left the clinic. For some reason, they are not able to "target" his radiation in the same manner as mine, so, he is getting "blasted." I really feel for him, especially since he doesn't have a feeding tube.

I expect, at some point, for my feeding tube to have to be swapped out for a new one. The surgeon said this one will either crack or clog and will have to be replaced. The one I have is marked "traction removal." That means the doc will put his foot on my chest and pull it out. While I am passed out, he will cram a new one in the hole and I will be as good as new!

I am in excellent condition as I get ready to resume treatments on Tuesday. I am rested, the mouth is healing, and Lortab continues to manage the pain. There are a lot of reasons I am doing as well as I am, the chief of which is answered prayer. I continue to get cards each week from people I don't know, but are friends of many of you. They tell us they are praying for my healing. Judy and I are genuinely humbled by the way you pray for us, as well as solicit the prayers of others. There is no doubt in my mind that God is answering those prayers. I ask, as we get back to treatment on Tuesday, that you continue your prayers for my healing, but also, please thank God for the prayer he has answered already. We are so thankful!

"Fight's On!!!"

Don

My radiation therapy was administered using a technique called Intensity Modulated Radiation Therapy, or IMRT. IMRT allows the radiation to be targeted very precisely to specific locations. The linear accelerator rotated around the table I was positioned on and made eight stops, hitting one or more of the three tumors at seven of the eight stops. The eighth stop hit the lymph nodes in the clavicle area, where the lymph nodes in the neck drain to.

Not everyone is able to receive IMRT[4], because of where the tumor is located, or perhaps structure is interfering with the targeting. Thus, some folks get "blasted," or blanketed, with radiation over an entire area. IMRT is the preferable means of delivery, because more radiation can be directed to specific areas and it spares tissue which does not need to be radiated.

Above I mentioned the gentleman who is being "blasted" due to the location of his tumors. Walt is another who received radiation in this manner. Walt literally has three-inch long burn scars behind his ears and down into his neck from where the radiation was administered.

We all know that a burn wound is probably one of the most painful injuries we can receive. When adding the external burns Walt experienced, along with what is "normal" now in terms of mouth pain, I have difficulty contemplating just how painful Walt's treatment was.

-----Original Message-----
From: G. Millon Plyler
Sent: Friday, May 26, 11:05 PM
To: Don Sublett
Subject: RE: Update #14

Thx for the update; keep the positive attitude. I am praying several times a day for you. Prayer works, as I have seen it numerous times. The Lord knows what He is doing!

I am off to bed, and you better, too, young fella! Good night.

Millon

-----Original Message-----
From: Don Sublett
Sent: Saturday, May 27, 8:30 AM
To: G. Millon Plyler
Subject: RE: Update #14

Millon,

It's easy to have a positive attitude when you feel as well as I do. I expect things might heat up a bit, since it all accumulates over time. Still, I am confident we are going to weather this better than the doctors indicated I would. Lots of factors, like I have iterated before: good health, nutrition, hydration, equipment; but it is mostly answered prayer. Just need to make sure God's hand is guiding the directing of the radiation as we move forward. I am concerned the cancer has had time to regenerate some during the break. The doctors don't seem particularly concerned that we have lost ground. I suppose we just have to wait and see.

Time to get back to my morning routine. Brush teeth with fluoride, take pain meds and wait 30 minutes before eating/drinking. Then, hit the feeding tube, swish with Gelclair, wait another 60 minutes before eating/drinking. It takes a long time to get the morning stuff taken care of. Don't know what I would do if I had to work.

Take care,

Don

-----Original Message-----
From: Glenn G.
Sent: Monday, May 29, 8:26 AM
To: Don Sublett
Subject: RE: Update #14

Hi Don,

It's encouraging to us to continue to receive these updates on your progress. Sounds as though you are "in good shape for the shape you're in." I know the Lord is looking out for you and Judy, both. I am reluctant to call, because I am afraid talking may be difficult, but just know you are regularly in our prayers and we are looking forward to your return to good health (and returning to our little church home group).

We really miss you. Hang in there and let us know if we can do anything at all.

Love you both!

Glenn and Nancy

-----Original Message-----
From: Don Sublett
Sent: Monday, May 29 8:55 AM
To: Glenn G.
Subject: RE: Update #14

Glenn and Nancy,

I am doing very well right now. The throat is still in good condition and the mouth is just about healed. It has been good to have little more than a week to re-gather my strength while not having any treatments, though I would have much preferred to press ahead and nail the cancer while we had it on the run. I start back with both chemo and radiation again, tomorrow, so we can finish the job of killing the cancer.

I, too, am looking forward to getting these next few weeks behind us so life can get back to whatever "normal" will be. I miss being with the church family, but I know that will change here before long. We do appreciate the concern and prayers. There is no doubt the prayers are being answered. Keep them going up, because we're not done yet!

Love you all,

Don

-----Original Message-----
From: Walt Leirer
Sent: Wednesday, May 31, 3:41 PM
To: Don Sublett
Subject: Re: Update #14

Hey Don,

I am surprised about them replacing your feeding tube. I had mine in for seven plus months.

Is that Gelclair an over the counter product? I would like to try some for the sore mouth I have all the time.

Thanks,

Walt

-----Original Message-----
From: Don Sublett
Sent: Wednesday, May 31, 5:46 PM
To: Walt Leirer
Subject: Re: Update #14

Walt,

Mine looks like it might have a weak spot in it. The surgeon told me yesterday we can cut it below there when/if it cracks and put another "throat" on it. That can be done a number of times, so it probably will not have to be replaced. That's not what I was told earlier, though.

Gelclair is a prescription medicine which has to be special ordered through a pharmacy. The prescription should be written for four boxes of 21 packets, which is about a 30-day supply (use three times daily, or less, if you don't need it that much). It might be worth a try for you to get it. It sure has helped my mouth sores tremendously. My mouth is just about clear after seven days of use.

Don

****

-----Original Message-----
From: Don Sublett
Sent: Monday, June 05, 7:14 PM
To: Support Group
Subject: Update #15

Good Evening, Friends!

I think I am starting to understand what the word "cumulative" means. It means you are going to get really, really tired toward the end of the week(s). Last Friday, I was pretty well-whipped, but managed to get quite a bit of my strength back over the weekend—just in time to start the drill again, today. Fortunately, I have not been driven down so far yet that I can't bounce back.

In spite of the sometimes physically weakening effects of the treatment, I remain in excellent condition. Blood counts are down some, but not enough to cause concern to any of the doctors. My weight loss fluctuates between ten and twelve pounds, and the doctors are comfortable with that. They don't want me to lose ten percent of my starting body weight, because losing that much would force them to reduce both the amount of chemo and radiation I am being given. I am pumping as many calories through the feeding tube daily as I can handle, which is somewhere between 2,000 - 2,400, but I am still hungry! Liquid foods may sustain, but they sure don't satisfy.

My mouth has healed nicely, but the combined effects of the chemo and radiation on the taste buds and saliva glands, as well as the medications I am taking, leave me unwilling to take solids by mouth. The throat is still pretty open, so I am able to drink fluids and take pills orally, but the taste of any food is utterly wicked. However, my sense of smell is still alive and well. It is so good I can smell the aromas in the food commercials on

TV! Do you realize how many food commercials there are on TV, especially when you are hungry?

My three doctors continue to be amazed at how well I am holding up and responding while under treatment. In fact, Dr. Bonanno (radiation) said last Thursday that he was going to make me the clinic's poster child. Dr. Prieto (chemo) seemed stunned today that I am still able to swallow. Dr. McMurphy (ENT) is also amazed I am this far into treatment and still having minimal pain, which is the case. Lortab continues to do the job and I hope it remains that way. Depending on who I listen to, pain has pretty much peaked. Or, I still have another level or two which I will experience. That will unfold as treatments progress, but I know where I stand in the matter. At present, I continue to be "comfortable."

Each doctor is extremely pleased at the cancer's response to the chemo and radiation. None can feel any signs of the cancerous nodes in the neck. Dr. Bonanno said today that the short term outlook is excellent, but he can't say anything regarding the long term (which I can understand). Dr. Bonnano also said he would not have imagined the cancerous nodes in the neck responding in such a significant way to treatment. Now, *that comment took me by surprise*! Evidently, not everyone responds as I have. I am tremendously blessed.

The end of treatment is starting to come into view. Two more rounds of chemo and 12 radiation treatments remain. I am convinced it is good doctors, good medicine, your prayers, and God's healing hands which have guided us thus far. Please hang in there with us these remaining days and continue those prayers! God loves you and Judy, and I do, too!

"Fight's On!!!"

Don

-----Original Message-----
From: Wanda Nobles
Sent: Monday, June 05, 7:30 PM
To: Don Sublett
Subject: Re: Update #15

Hey, Poster Child!

Well, if the doctors are surprised at how well you are handling the treatments and how well you are responding to them, then they just don't know the power of God the way we do! It doesn't surprise me at all, although it thrills me to no end to see you are doing so well, and also to see the power of our Almighty Father at work in you! Praise God!

Judy seemed to be doing well yesterday and it was great to see Michael again! I am sure it is a joy to have him around! I still think he's such a sweet "little boy"! Don't tell him that!

Yes, Buddy, fight's on, but the outcome is not in doubt, as far as I am concerned. That cancer is fighting a losing battle in you! Thanks to God, the victory is assured!

Continuing in prayer,

Wanda

-----Original Message-----
From: Don Sublett
Sent: Monday, June 05, 7:46 PM
To: Wanda Nobles
Subject: Re: Update #15

Wanda,

There is no doubt that God has answered a lot of prayer along the way and continues to do so. I tell my doctors there are good doctors and good medicine at work, and that *a lot* of people are praying for me. None of them deny His hand is also at work. They all seem to be believers, too. I like that. I am very confident we will kill the cancer and I understand why they can't be overly committal about that.

On top of everything else, Judy came down with shingles. She is being treated and is showing signs of improvement each day. We are told it will take about three weeks to knock the shingles out, so she is working on it.

It is good to have Michael here. I think it is a little bit of a rest for him, since I am not requiring a lot of "maintenance." Not like I thought I would when we planned all of this out. I am certainly thankful for that!

We sure do appreciate having our "prayer warriors" at work. I know God loves that, too!

We love you!

Don

-----Original Message-----
From: G. Millon Plyler
Sent: Monday, June 05, 7:48 PM
To: Don Sublett
Subject: RE: Update #15

It is great to see the Lord's work unfold. I prayed for you while walking this afternoon; came in and got your e-mail. Prayers do get answered.

Keep fighting!

Millon

-----Original Message-----
From: Don Sublett
Sent: Monday, June 05, 7:58 PM
To: G. Millon Plyler
Subject: RE: Update #15

Millon,

There is no doubt God is answering prayer. I can't explain the fact I am doing so well any other way. What makes it so nice is there are so many folks praying for me that I have no idea how many there are. I just know there are a lot.

We are looking forward to getting this behind us and moving into the healing mode, so I can eat again. I had no idea food, or anything else for that matter, could taste so bad. I hope you never have to go through anything like this. I wouldn't wish it on my worst enemy.

Sure do appreciate the prayers, and I know that you *will* keep them up. That means a lot.

Don

-----Original Message-----
From: Linda Allen
Sent: Monday, June 05, 7:34 PM
To: Don Sublett
Subject: Re: Update #15

Hi Don.

It was good to hear from you. You sound like you are the model patient! I guess they do want to use you for the poster child. I have been in St. Louis since last week, with the grandchildren. I will be home Wed. Take care of yourself and *pump* those calories! Love to you and Judy!

Linda

-----Original Message-----
From: Don Sublett
Sent: Monday, June 05, 8:22 PM
To: Linda Allen
Subject: Re: Update #15

Linda,

I think being a good patient is part of it, but I do have good doctors looking after me, and God is looking after all of us. Pretty tough combination to beat, and that is making all the difference. We are looking forward to the time we can get together again and break some *real* bread. I am eating to live at the moment. It will be nice to turn things around before long.

Love you all!

Don

-----Original Message-----
From: Gilda Laird
Sent: Monday, June 05, 8:17 PM
To: Don Sublett
Subject: Re: Update #15

Don,

I am praising God right now for the obvious answer to prayers on your behalf. I am just thrilled at how you have responded to treatment, your continued good blood count levels, and

your ability to deal with the obvious pain associated with treatment. *I love it* when God shows off,
don't you? Hang in there! The finish line is near!

Much love,

Gilda

-----Original Message-----
From: Don Sublett
Sent: Monday, June 05, 9:20 PM
To: Gilda Laird
Subject: Re: Update #15

Gilda,

God is taking good care of us and I know
that will continue. We certainly have a lot to be
thankful for. Just continue to pray for us. I know
you will.

Love you guys!

Don

-----Original Message-----
From: Mike Bagwell
Sent: Monday, June 05, 8:28 PM
To: Don Sublett
Subject: RE: Update #15

Don,

That is wonderful news! You sound great!
Glad to hear you are doing so well. You will be finishing the treatments before you know it. As you
said, the cumulative effects are adding up, both
in the wear and tear on you, but more impor-

tantly, in the cancer cells. How are they planning to evaluate the cancer when you are finished?

Take care and have a good, solid week.

Mike

-----Original Message-----
From: Don Sublett
Sent: Monday, June 05, 9:44 PM
To: Mike Bagwell
Subject: RE: Update #15

Mike,

Knowing what has happened to the nodes in the neck tells me that if they are hitting the cancer in the tongue, which seven of the eight radiation stops do, the same thing almost has to be happening to the cancer there. I am pretty confident we will get a good report when this thing is over.

Six weeks after the last treatment they will do a combined CT/PET scan to see if there is any sign of cancer remaining. If there is, they will most likely go after it surgically.

Keep those prayers coming!

Don

-----Original Message-----
From: Jane Keller
Sent: Monday, June 05, 8:34 PM
To: Don Sublett
Subject: Re: Update #15

We are so happy you continue to respond so well to treatment. Have the children been coming to help? Does Judy take you to treatments, and is she doing ok, as well? We continue to include you in every prayer and we all know that is why you are responding so well—prayers from all over the world on your behalf! Are you able to go to church, or are you able, but don't go to avoid all those germs out there? Joe is getting a new boat so, when you are feeling better, we can all go out and celebrate!

Loving all of you,

Jane and Joe

-----Original Message-----
From: Don Sublett
Sent: Monday, June 05, 9:59 PM
To: Jane Keller
Subject: Re: Update #15

Jane (and Joe),

We, too, are thrilled at the way things are going. God is most definitely leading the charge here, and we are so thankful He is.

I am still driving myself to treatment. The Lortab makes me a bit drowsy at times, but it is nothing I can't fight through. If I have to bump up my dosage I will not be driving. Judy goes with me sometimes, but mainly just for company.

We have had someone here for the last three weeks and Michael is here this week. Les will be coming on the 11th and leaving on the 18th. Then, Judy's oldest sister (Yvonne) and her husband will come back, if needed. They were here last week, too. Michael and Les then follow them back, if circumstances warrant. The extra help hasn't really been needed, but we planned it on the basis of the scenario the doctors initially gave us. Obviously, things are a bit different than they projected.

I could go to church, but I am staying out of large crowds. The blood is low in a few components, but still in pretty good shape overall. The docs and nurses tell me to avoid the crowds. So, as part of being the "good patient," I am following their orders. However, it will be good to get back with the church family.

There is still a lot of tissue which will die over the next couple of weeks and I am going to be a bit "sun sensitive" for quite a while. However, we will keep the boat ride on our list of "things to do."

You are right about people all over the world praying for us. They literally are. Without our "prayer warriors," I don't know where we would be. We are so thankful for our friends who know there is power in prayer!

We love and appreciate you all so very much!

Don

-----Original Message-----
From: Dan Willcox
Sent: Tuesday, June 06, 7:39 AM
To: Don Sublett
Subject: Re: Update #15

Dear Mr. Sublett,

Thanks for the updates! I'm sorry I have not responded more. Please know you are in our thoughts and prayers constantly.

I must tell you, I am not surprised at all by your positive response to treatment. I have absolute certainty that God is fixing it. Whether He is doing it with his hand directly, or his hand on the Doc's, with the meds—who cares? Either way works and it is Him doing it.

Knowing what you are going through and having watched Laurie deal with a similar struggle, I have come to tearful, painful, sometimes angry and, ultimately, peaceful, absolute understanding of why Great people are "allowed" to face such difficult things. That understanding is, it helps us all to remember what is important in this life, which in my words, are love God, and love all people. The rest really doesn't add up to a hill of beans.

Make it a great day!

Love,

Dan

-----Original Message-----
From: Don Sublett
Sent: Tuesday, June 06, 8:49 AM
To: Dan Willcox
Subject: Re: Update #15

Dan,

Don't be sorry for not responding more via e-mail. You have a life to live and celebrate, and a family to support. I know support has come via your prayers and God's response to them, through whatever means He has chosen. I have benefited more than folks will ever realize, or I will ever be able to convey.

I have never asked God, "Why me?" throughout this entire experience. Stuff just happens and you must deal with it. The cancer has certainly increased my faith and understanding of God's grace. Perhaps that was a lesson needed. Regardless, it has been a powerful lesson learned and reinforced by our friends.

Today is a wonderful day and tomorrow will be, too! Judy and I love and appreciate you guys tremendously!

Don

-----Original Message-----
From: Darlene Morris
Sent: Tuesday, June 06, 8:12 AM
To: Don Sublett
Subject: Re: Update #15

Dear Don and Judy,

My first response is "How amazing!" and yet, that is silly, because that is exactly what we have all been praying for. We do serve a God who continually amazes us. Isn't that wonderful? We are thrilled and will continue to pray.

In Him,

Darlene

-----Original Message-----
From: Don Sublett
Sent: Tuesday, June 06, 1:33 PM
To: Darlene Morris
Subject: Re: Update #15

Darlene,

In a sense, it is amazing, but I don't think God minds us being amazed at His goodness, sometimes. I think there is a smile on His face, just as there is on mine.

We surely appreciate the prayers and know they will continue!

Love,

Don

-----Original Message-----
From: Denise G.
Sent: Tuesday, June 06, 8:13 AM
To: Don Sublett
Subject: Re: Update #15

Hi Don and Judy,

At my request, Leslie W. has been forwarding your dialogue to me. Both of you have been in my prayers. I have to say, I feel you are more uplifting to those of us who read your updates than we are to you. Your faith in God is ever present and the power of the Holy Spirit is felt. The anointing which we don't quite understand as humans is God's gift to us for having faith that He knows all and we are to simply be willing to do as He says—no questions asked!

Of course, over the years I have known you, even if we might not always agree, there has never been any doubt in my mind that your faith in God is ever present. He is truly blessing you, your family, other Christians, and who knows how many others who come upon your writings. I will continually pray for your complete healing and for your family's strength.

Judy, I cannot imagine what you have gone through, being sick, yourself, and the wondering you must be experiencing. I know when Elton fell off the roof last year, as soon as I found out, I started praying—even without knowing his status. That incident was short lived; it's nothing in comparison to what you are going through. God bless you both.

Love,

Denise

P.S.: Don't feel you need to respond to me personally. I know time constraints, weakness, and so on are ever present. Just know we love you!

-----Original Message-----
From: Don Sublett
Sent: Tuesday, June 06, 1:53 PM
To: Denise G.
Subject: Re: Update #15

Denise,

I really appreciate your interest in staying up with my cancer as treatment progresses. I will add you to my update list, if that is ok? That way you will not have to rely on Leslie for them. In a sense, it is therapeutic for me to send the updates out. As I write them, it forces me to keep my head "in the game."

Many, just as you, have told me the updates are uplifting and encouraging to them. I must say to you that responses such as yours are *extremely* encouraging to me! Those are "positive vibes" which reinforce my "positive vibes." Also, it is nice to know people are involved and actively praying for my healing. I am convinced there are hundreds, maybe thousands of people all over the world praying for us. God is clearly hearing and answering those prayers.

I have always tried to live my faith. Sometimes I have done a reasonably good job and other times not. It would be a terrible thing to profess to have faith and then for that faith to fail when it is most needed. I am just glad I have had a chance to grow in faith over the years and God is allowing my faith to become even greater. It has certainly provided every assurance I could ask for in dealing with the cancer.

Judy has hung in there really well. In a sense, it is probably tougher on her at times than it is on me. You always hate to see somebody you love in trouble. No matter what the trouble might be.

We truly appreciate the prayers and I hope I am able to adequately portray in my updates that God is hearing and answering those prayers. I think He has a big smile on His face—just as I do, mine.

We love you!

Don

****

-----Original Message-----
From: Don Sublett
Sent: Sunday, June 11, 6:36 PM
To: Support Group
Subject: Update #16

Good Evening All,

I sit here on the cusp of the last full week of treatment, very thankful the end of chemo and radiation is starting to come into view! It would be very easy to declare victory and start jumping for joy at the prospect, but I know there is still a lot of cancer killing which will be done. It is apparent once again that we are killing cells in the mouth, throat, and tongue. That is most certainly good to know! We will let things continue to take their course over the remaining days, with full knowledge God is in control.

My physical condition continues to be excellent and I remain very comfortable, as the Lortab is still doing its job in managing the pain. There is quite a bit of increased sensitivity in the mouth and this is apparently the normal progression. Previously, Dr. McMurphy (ENT) told me my mouth will be raw, bloody, and very painful by the time we are done. However, I think this was before the Gelclair came into the mix. I will be very surprised if the mouth deteriorates to that point after seeing how the Gelclair has worked thus far, but I have bumped up the amount of Lortab in each dose just a bit to take the edge off. Meanwhile, I remain considerably under the max amount of Lortab I can take in each dose, and the number of doses I can take each day.

I have one more round of chemo, which will be given on Tuesday and Wednesday, and eight more radiation treatments remaining. There will be some changes during the last five radiation treatments. In order to salvage as much of the saliva glands as possible, they will switch from protons to electrons when treating the areas where the saliva glands are located. (Electrons don't penetrate as deeply into the tissue.) I sincerely appreciate this effort on the part of my doctors to salvage the glands, because "dry mouth" is one of the most annoying after-effects of the treatment. I am curious if the change in just five treatments will be enough to make much of a difference, but I will take everything they offer, so long as it doesn't impact the killing of the cancer.

Also, they will give the maximum amount of radiation possible to the base of the tongue those last five treatments. That appears to be a fair amount more than what I am presently receiving. It is for this reason I feel a need to keep my optimism cautiously in check, because I know there is still time for things to heat up substantially. For some reason, Dr. McMurphy's eyes literally lit up when I told her the plan is to bump up the radiation to "70 Gray." I hope it is because she thinks this will be a good thing and not because she is sadistic!

As we get to near the end of treatments, I continue to marvel at the way God has blessed me—and my family—throughout this entire experience. It is so obvious God is hearing your prayers and is answering them every single day. For that, I am so very grateful! I am humbled by God's love, grace, and mercy.

As I look back, I have spent a large part of my life trying to be actively involved in the church and the Lord's work. However, I don't think I have ever, in any really significant way, worn Christ's cause on my sleeve (so to speak). As so many of you have told me, "You have a story to tell." I can only agree. I do have a story to tell, and I hope with whatever of my life remains, I can do a more effective job of telling that story. We are blessed people and our God is an awesome God!

"Fight's On!!!"

Don

-----Original Message-----
From: Brenda Fahey
Sent: Sunday, June 11, 6:57 PM
To: Don Sublett
Subject: Re: Update #16

Good evening, my dear Brother,

A story to tell? To be sure! And you are doing it in an amazing way with each of your updates. Thank you for sharing so much and in such a positive way. I know Mom and Dad would be (and are) proud of you. Tears come to my eyes as I think of just how proud they would be of you. The kind of faith that you are proclaiming doesn't come from a book or any "book-learnin'" you have had. It comes from a very personal relationship with the Lord. I stand amazed at how anyone can get through this—or the death of a spouse—without a personal relationship with Him.

Tell Leslie, "Hi," for me. I guess she is there by now. Tell Judy, "Hi," too. I hope she is enjoying her time off.

God bless!

Sis

P.S.: Just curious—what has been the hardest thing through this journey for you? The original diagnosis, the surgeries you have had, the uncertainty of the future? I am not sure why I am asking—just curious, I guess.

-----Original Message-----
From: Don Sublett
Sent: Sunday, June 11, 8:13 PM
To: Brenda Fahey
Subject: Re: Update #16

Evenin' Sis,

I am glad my faith has both held and strengthened through this experience. I agree that I don't know how folks without Christ in their life get through life's most difficult hardships.

As to the toughest part, that is really difficult to say. Probably getting the initial diagnosis and having it sink in. Once you are confronted with the facts and set your mind on how you will respond, it is then a matter of following through with what you have decided. I might, after a little more thought on that, revise it some, but that is what comes to mind first.

Les got here just fine and she and Judy are at home group this evening. Should be getting back shortly.

Love you,

Don

-----Original Message-----
From: Jerry McCormick
Sent: Monday, June 12, 5:27 AM
To: Don Sublett
Subject: Re: Update #16

Brother Don,

Thanks for adding me to your e-mail report list. As I just read your "Update #16," I had to think whether you are the patient or the doctor. You sound so clinical and removed from the pain. No doubt, this is God's blessing and peace in your life. Janet and I were at the Niceville church two Sundays ago and we were going to come visit you. Cathy S. said I should not go since I have never had chicken pox. Your update report just flows with the confidence you have in God. That encourages me and others. All is well with me and my family. It has been a year since my bypass and the Lord continues to bless me. I hope Judy is doing well with the shingles.

Your brother in Christ,

Jerry

-----Original Message-----
From: Don Sublett
Sent: Monday, June 12, 8:59 AM
To: Jerry McCormick
Subject: Re: Update #16

Jerry,

Once hit with a major setback, you have to determine how you will respond, as you well know. I have mentioned to others and I'll also mention it to you: It would be a terrible thing to have your faith fail when it was needed the most. God has so wonderfully answered many prayers on my behalf that it is astounding. He has allowed my faith to increase through this time and I try to convey that to folks I come into contact with, as well as in my updates. I have every confidence God will use the doctors and medicine to heal me. However, if we can't kill the cancer in the body, I still can't lose, because Jesus is my Savior. Still, looking at how the cancer has responded in the neck, I can't believe we are getting any other response in the tongue.

It is especially obvious that He has blessed me when I look at others with the same cancer I have and how they are responding to treatment. I don't know how they will make it through to the end without being hospitalized. Their doctors didn't do a good job prepping them—or maybe they didn't listen—and I think most of them don't have a very strong faith in God's healing power. I pray for them, too.

Appreciate you wanted to come and visit, but I have been holding off on having company for a while now, due to dropping blood counts and trying to minimize the risk of infection. Just trying to be smart and follow the doctors' orders and recommendations. We may stop in and pay you a visit, sometime. It has been a while since we have been up I-65 any distance. You are certainly welcome here anytime. I hope and trust the Lord will continue to bless each of us!

In Christ!

Don

-----Original Message-----
From: G. Millon Plyler
Sent: Monday, June 12, 6:56 PM
To: Don Sublett
Subject: RE: Update #16

Thx for the good report. I knew God would come into play in this and you are seeing that first hand. Don, who knows? Maybe this is the Lord's way of using your illness to get you to espouse your feelings and bring others to Him? I got you in prayer tonight during my walk and I will say another at bedtime. Stay out of Alberto's way!

Fight on my friend,

Millon

-----Original Message-----
From: Don Sublett
Sent: Monday, June 12, 8:24 PM
To: G. Millon Plyler
Subject: RE: Update #16

Millon,

He has certainly opened my eyes through this experience, and probably some others, too. We know for a fact there is power in prayer. God has shown us that time and again throughout this experience.

I am certainly looking forward to getting the next week or so behind me so the healing (and eating) can begin. I am pumping all the calories I can through the feeding tube and my stomach is growling. Ha! I am still not eating any solids by mouth. Food tastes horrible and there is no sense tearing the throat up. I honestly don't know how folks without the feeding tube make it through this treatment. I think I would starve to death. We don't know how long it will take for the taste buds to recover, but I am hoping not very long. I will probably continue using the feeding tube as the main source for nutrition for at least two or three weeks while the throat heals.

(Hurricane) Alberto is no threat to us up here, but we wouldn't mind being on the fringe of it. We could sure use the rain. We are down about a foot for the year.

Stay safe. Sure appreciate the prayers!

Don

****

From: Don Sublett
Sent: Thursday, June 15, 9:10 AM
To: Dr. McMurphy
Subject: Where We Stand...and a Concern

Dr. Mac,

I continue to progress in excellent fashion. However, some adjustments are being made to my diet which I think will cause me to lose some weight.

Chemo is done and I start the last of five radiation treatments today in San Destin, using electrons in two areas to try and salvage some of the saliva glands. Radiation will be boosted to "70 Gray." I have a *noticeable increase* in sensitivity in the mouth and have boosted my Lortab accordingly. (Mid-tongue and other areas are white from the radiation and turn to that green phlegm that sloughs off when I rinse.) I am now taking Lortab in doses of 18ml 3x day and 22ml at night. I am assuming max dose is/will be 25ml x 6, so I have a way to go. However, I sense I will eat this up pretty quickly by the time we get to the weekend. I hope I am mistaken. If that is the case, is it reasonable to have the next level of pain medication on the shelf, here at the house, if needed? I don't want to be illegal or unethical in trying to go this route, but just continue to be as proactive as we have been all along. If it is needed, I will use it. If not, I won't.

Dr. Prieto is gone, but said he expected you to take over the case regarding pain management and that he would brief you. I don't know if he did or not, but I have every confidence in you. Heck, I may be getting paranoid at this point, because the pain has been managed so well and I just can't believe it is going to continue so well. If you think I am all wet, don't hesitate to tell me.

As always, thanks for your time.

Don

-----Original Message-----
From: Dr. McMurphy
Sent: Thursday, June 15, 1:35 PM
To: Don Sublett
Subject: RE: Where We Stand...and a Concern

Hello! I put in for the patches. Let me know if they help. You may not need the Lortab with them, but can take them at the same time. Beware of constipation.

Only five to go. Whoo-hoo!

Dr. Mac

-----Original Message-----
From: Don Sublett
Sent: Thursday, June 15, 4:45 PM
To: Dr. McMurphy
Subject: RE: Where We Stand...and a Concern

Thanks, Dr. Mac!

I went out for the 31st treatment and their phone lines were down. They get their dosimeter feeds from Fort Myers into the machine, in the office. No treatment today, which I hated. Will go back tomorrow and suppose to finish up on Thursday, next week. Will keep you apprised.

Thanks again!

Don

****

-----Original Message-----
From: Don Sublett
Sent: Tuesday, June 20, 10:14 PM
To: Support Group
Subject: Update #17

Good Evening, Everyone!

We are two days from wrapping up treatment for this cancer. We would have wrapped up tomorrow, but they were unable to treat last Thursday due to "phone line" problems in Fort Myers. It seems they get their dosimeter feeds and other info into the linear accelerator from there—quite a complex operation, and that is an obvious understatement.

I remain in excellent condition. My health is good, though I don't have a whole lot of energy. I have lost about 15 pounds since we began and a lot of that is muscle mass, not that I was all that muscular to begin with. The body uses a lot of its stores in fighting the cancer and the muscle is just one source. The nutritionist, Lt Schwebel, had me cut out the protein powder I was using, due to the fact I had too much protein in the blood. This change costs me close to 500 calories a day. Though I can make up some of the calorie loss with juices, there is no way I can see to make up the entire amount. So, it is likely I will continue to drop a bit of weight until I can get back to more of a normal diet.

Pain has slightly increased since we entered these last five treatments, in the "boost" phase. My mouth is a mess—large sores on the sides of the tongue, blisters, swelling, dead tissue—but is far less a mess than what is normally experienced due to radiation. The Gelclair has done a marvelous job of keeping the mouth problems in check, to the extent possible, and the Lortab is not the "baby pain med" as some have described it. (Les, give your bio-chemist friend a *big hug*!)

A corresponding bump in the Lortab has handled the increased pain very adequately. Dr. Mac (ENT) went ahead and prescribed the Duragesic (Fentanyl) patches in case the higher radiation caused a significant increase in pain. I don't expect to have to use the patch, but certainly will if warranted.

Judy and I met with Dr. Bonanno today after my treatment. He is very pleased, as are we, with the cancer's response (at least in the nodes in the neck) to the chemo and radiation. Though there is no way to say definitively that the cancer in the tongue is killed until after the CT/PET scan on 3 Aug., he seemed optimistic I will have a good scan. I think we *will all* be very surprised if I don't, but that remains a possibility. Ultimately, it is in God's hands.

Dr. Bonnano said my taste buds should regenerate over the next three months. Some tastes may not come back and others might be different. Others I am aware of have had good response regarding the return of the taste buds. I just look forward to the time when something tastes different than what it tastes like now. Ha!

In our discussion today, Dr. Bonnano again emphasized one reason I have fared so well is the fact I began in good health and have been able to maintain it. The feeding tube has been key to this. He mentioned that very few people will opt for a feeding tube and said he has a hard time understanding that. Perhaps the doctors don't do a good enough job emphasizing the potential need for it, or people aren't listening when potential obstacles are explained. I don't know either. However, I do know you need to take advantage of every possible option to increase the odds in your favor when faced with decisions affecting your treatment for cancer, or any other disease. If you think there is a health problem brewing, then deal with it promptly. Don't drag your feet!

Every doctor and technician tells me what an anomaly I am for someone with base-of-tongue cancer. My skin didn't even burn from the radiation! As mentioned before, I have had good doctors, good medicine, and good advice from everyone involved in my treatment. I have also benefited from the advances made in cancer treatment, particularly the combination therapies, administration of radiation, and chemistry such as Gelclair.

For nearly fifty-nine years, I never had a storm cloud in my life—nothing but pure sunshine. Then, this cancer showed up. I don't know if this particular cancer will ultimately kill me, if it will be another cancer as a result of this one, or if it will be something else entirely. However, I do know I will not live forever, here. This experience has demonstrated that very dramatically to me and has also made me even more keenly aware of what Christ did for each one of us on the cross.

Ultimately, the credit for the way I have managed to make it through treatment goes to God. I know that throughout this entire experience God has blessed a pretty ordinary guy in extraordinary ways, because of your prayers and

His love, and grace. I am so very humbled and appreciative.

Fight's On!!!

Don

-----Original Message-----
From: Billy T.
Sent: Tuesday, June 20, 4:06 PM
To: Don Sublett
Subject: Checking In

Hello Don:

I have been tracking your health through Jane Keller and the church bulletin. However, I wanted to write and say you have been on my mind and in my prayers for some time. Please give me an update on your treatment and how you are doing.

In 2002, I was diagnosed with prostate cancer and shortly after had my prostate removed. There is a tendency to cry out to God, "Why me?" Then, I read in John 9:3 where Jesus said the man was born blind "so that the work of God might be displayed in his life." I believe this is equally true for people like us, who are stricken with disease.

Warm regards and much love to Judy.

Stay in touch,

Billy T

-----Original Message-----
From: Don Sublett
Sent: Tuesday, June 20, 6:46 PM
To: Billy T.
Subject: Checking In

Billy,

Good to hear from you!

Things continue to go *extremely* well with me. The treatment for this cancer is supposed to be one of the most difficult and painful a person can endure. However, my response has been far different and better than I suspect anyone could have imagined. Most folks with tongue cancer at this stage have been on morphine and/or Fentanyl for quite a time already. I am still on Lortab and it looks like I probably will finish up on Lortab. It is very clear to me that God has heard and answered an awful lot of prayer on our behalf these last few months, and is continuing to do so. There is no other answer.

I have two more radiation appointments, tomorrow and Thursday, and that finishes treatment. I will have a CT/PET scan on 3 Aug. My ENT will use the scans for diagnostic purposes to see where we go from here. My radiation oncologist told Judy and me, today, that we should be gratified by the response the cancer has shown to the chemo and radiation. We certainly are! The cancerous nodes in the neck are gone and I suspect he is inferring the same thing has happened to the cancer in the tongue. We will know the answer to that better after the scan.

I know the normal tendency when you encounter problems is like you describe. However, I have never questioned God as to, *"Why me?"* I don't believe I have even "thought" that particular question. I know things happen in life. Generally, because of actions on our part. When told I had cancer, I accepted that fact and acknowledged I had to deal with it. I also acknowledged it was something I would not be able to deal with on my own, particularly the painful/difficult course of treatment I would undergo. So, I sought my refuge in God and strength in Christ. Needless to say, God has protected, blessed, and healed. I am truly humbled by His grace and love, shown me throughout this experience. It has been remarkable. I can't imagine how people without God in their lives survive something like this, but I know they do. I certainly have a story to tell and trust God wants that story told.

We have had a lot of family here throughout my treatments, thinking they would be needed as caregivers. However, they have been able to visit instead. Les came from D.C. and spent a week. Michael came from Katy, TX, and also spent a week with us. Then, we've had some of Judy's family here, too. I don't know who is in next week, or if anyone will come, since I am doing so well. Though, I do know the kids and their families will all probably be here, together, sometime in July.

I will continue to "cook and burn" for another six weeks, and the actual healing in the throat will not begin for at least three weeks. I will have about a six week recovery period between now and the scans, in Aug. Please continue to keep us in your prayers.

Don

I had finished my chemo the week prior and still had the two radiation treatments mentioned above remaining. Dr. Gorrebeeck offered another dose of the Docetaxol and Cisplatin in conjunction with those two remaining treatments. When that option was offered, I *immediately* declined. I'd had all of the chemo I wanted and all I wanted at that moment was to be done!

Looking back, that was not a wise decision, even though I know now that declining the additional chemo was not detrimental to my outcome, but *it could have been.* I had endured the chemo to that point and I should have endured one more round. I was not thinking clearly when I declined.

-----Original Message-----
From: Sanford Flach
Sent: Wednesday, June 21, 5:31 AM
To: Don Sublett
Subject: Re: Update #17

Hang in there, Don. It is good to hear you are doing so well and are at the end of your treatment, already. By this time in my treatment, I was on the transdermal patch, which started at 25mg, and then 50mg, and then 75mg. My dosage ultimately got up to 100mg. Of course, I was the one who failed to get a feeding tube. In looking back on the pain I endured, if I had to do it over, I would definitely have gotten a feeding tube. I hope you continue to do well and that you come into complete remission.

I am still doing well. I had a CT scan about three weeks ago and it came out fine. I still have some difficulty swallowing, but my ENT seems to think it is from the scarring and the fluid swelling in the tissues in the front of my neck. When I wake in the morning, my neck is more swollen than later in the day. He attributes this to gravity, as the lymph node area drains better when vertical than when lying down. I view this swelling as a very minor thing when compared to the cancer I had one year ago.

We will continue to keep you in our prayers.

Sanford

-----Original Message-----
From: Don Sublett
Sent: Wednesday, June 21, 9:16 AM
To: Sanford Flach
Subject: Re: Update #17

Sanford,

Good to hear from you and to know things continue to go well with you.

I marvel at how well things have gone for me to this point, especially when I think about you and the other guys I know who have undergone the same treatment. Then, there are those I am presently in treatment with. They are following your path, too. If somebody has an answer other than God, they would have a hard time making a case for it, as far as I am concerned.

I don't know what lingering effects I will have. At present, the throat seems to be pretty well open. I am still able to swallow most of my daily pills without a problem. I take a horse pill, called Zovirax, as a preventive, and it tried to hang in the throat with me one day. So, I now crush that one and push it through the feeding tube. No sense in forcing things if you don't have to.

I continue to drink small amounts of water and swallow as much daily as I can, in order to keep the throat exercised. I think by not forcing things down the throat, it has managed to pretty much stay intact throughout. Not irritating the throat has helped keep the pain levels down, too. This may stand me in good stead as the healing progresses and I start eating again. I wish I could say I had this all figured out well in advance, but it has been pretty much "step and stumble" along the way, with a little common sense on the side.

I believe I mentioned they are trying to salvage some of the saliva glands for me. Treatments 31 and 32 didn't hit them at all and these last three have them being hit with electrons in the area. I sure hope we reap some success from that approach.

God has certainly blessed me during this more than I ever imagined He would. It is because of people like you who believe in Him and in the power of prayer. I will continue to keep you in prayer as we move forward, as well.

Drop a line or give a call anytime. I really enjoy chatting with you!

Don

-----Original Message-----
From: Penny Bagwell.
Sent: Wednesday, June 21, 12:18 PM
To: Don Sublett
Subject: So glad your news continues to be positive

We are so glad you continue to get good news. I know God has a purpose for you. We are encouraged by your notes. I hope you attempt, in some way, to publish your journal. I think you could impact so many lives, as you have touched each one of us you have shared your journal with. We continue to keep you and Judy in our prayers and pray you continue with good results. Thank you for sharing.

Penny

-----Original Message-----
From: Don Sublett
Sent: Wednesday, June 21, 1:35 PM
To: Penny Bagwell.
Subject: So glad your news continues to be positive

Penny,

Thanks so much for the kind words. It is the prayers which have made all the difference in the world. We still have to get through the diagnostic tests in August, but I am confident that with God in control, things will be just fine.

As to publishing, others have suggested the same thing, but I haven't a clue regarding what might be involved. It could be something I look into after everything is said and done.

We really appreciate the continued prayers!

Love you all!

Don

-----Original Message-----
From: Paula Willcox
Sent: Thursday, June 22, 6:32 AM
To: Don Sublett
Subject: Re: Update #17

Last one! Praise the Lord! Hooray for you...

Love,

Paula

-----Original Message-----
From: Don Sublett
Sent: Thursday, June 22, 8:19 AM
To: Paula Willcox
Subj: Re: Update #17

Paula,

We are so grateful for the love and prayers of our good friends! Couldn't have made it without people calling on the Lord on our behalf!
Love you bunches!

Don

-----Original Message-----
From: Ed Ferrell
Sent: Thursday, June 22, 10:58 AM
To: Don Sublett
Subject: Home stretch!

Don,

I want to thank you for all your inspirational e-mail progress reports. I plan to send them to my son, in Tucson, who works with the Indian tribe and cancer patients. We always miss you at the Wed. night services, but remember you in prayer! Ron's message was very interesting last night and we had a good "crowd."
I know you will be so glad to be finished with the treatments and be able to go into "recovery mode." You have certainly done well under the circumstances.
Keeping you and Judy in our prayers. We love you.

Ed & Sandy

-----Original Message-----
From: Don Sublett
Sent: Thursday, June 22, 12:34 PM
To: Ed Ferrell
Subject: Home stretch!

Ed and Sandy,

This turkey is fried. We just got back from the last radiation treatment. Now we will soon begin to enter the healing phase. It will be quite slow, because the chemo and radiation will continue to work for several weeks yet. Actual healing will not begin for two or three weeks, but at least we are not pouring more gasoline on the fire.

Appreciate the thoughts and prayers, and look forward to getting back into the family in the next couple of weeks, or so.

Love you all!

Don

-----Original Message-----
From: Wanda Nobles
Sent: Sunday, June 25, 10:16 PM
To: Don Sublett
Subject: Good to See You!

Hey there!

Just wanted you to know how great it was to see you today! You were definitely a sight for sore eyes! I hope you don't think I am a real sap when I tell you I kept getting choked up sitting behind you this morning, just thinking about how grateful I was to God that you were able to be there, and thinking how wonderful it must feel to you, to be back in worship service communing with your brothers and sisters again. We have all missed you so much.

Hope you didn't wear yourself out too much! By the way, you look great!

Love you,

Wanda

-----Original Message-----
From: Don Sublett
Sent: Monday, June 26 9:19 AM
To: Wanda Nobles
Subject: Good to See You!

Wanda,

It was good to be back with the church family yesterday. Probably should have waited a week, but I just needed to get back. My eyes kind of misted up a couple of times during the service, as I reflected on the last several weeks. God has blessed me incredibly.

My energy level is good and will only get better, especially when I can get back to a normal diet. I hope that can begin happening in the next ten days or so. As soon as the mouth heals I will start making the change. My mouth healed quite a bit during my 11-day break, and I expect (hope) the same thing will happen now. It shouldn't take much longer than that.

The next hurdle is the CT/PET scan, on Aug 3rd. Once we see what that says, we will know where we stand. Still need those prayers!

Love you all, too!

Don

****

From: Don Sublett
Sent: Wednesday, July 05, 7:31 AM
To: Dr. McMurphy
Subject: Infection???

Dr. Mac,

I am concerned I have developed an infection in the face and it is moving into the neck. The swollen area—halfway up the cheek on each side, and the lower lip—is getting larger each day. I assume there are still some lymph nodes in the neck and it appears one on the right side is swollen. I thought I felt the same thing on the left side, yesterday, but can't seem to find the node this morning. Shouldn't the swelling be going down instead of increasing, if the last radiation was two weeks ago?

I have a 1:20 appointment with my Primary Care Manager, today, at Hurlburt, in case you are too busy to address my concern today.

Thank you so much.

Don

-----Original Message-----
From: Dr. McMurphy
Sent: Wednesday, July 05, 7:53 AM
To: Don Sublett
Subject: RE: Infection???

Mr. Sublett,

No infection. You are finally behaving like you are supposed to. Seriously, we expect swelling, redness, and pain of the skin—especially in the sites of the ports. Remember, the radiation keeps working

DON SUBLETT

for up to six weeks after you complete treatment. With the Diflucan and Zovirax, it is unlikely to be an infection. I would give Dr. Bonnano a call and see if he agrees. Keep your chin up!

Dr. Mac

-----Original Message-----
From: Don Sublett
Sent: Wednesday, July 05, 9:23 AM
To: Dr. McMurphy
Subject: RE: Infection???

Dr. Mac,

Why do I have to be normal?

I am not in any pain, though still taking the Lortab. However, the back of the lower gums certainly have some pain in them when touched with the tongue. I know they were hammered by the radiation.

The tongue sores are almost healed. Another day or two, I think. Once the tongue is clear, I plan to begin transitioning to a normal diet, hoping the taste buds soon begin to reappear. Also, I will cease taking the Diflucan and Zovirax at that time. Dr. Prieto said to cease the Zovirax at the end of treatment, but I have continued taking it. Dr. Bonnano said to take the Diflucan until the mouth healed.

I do have a couple decent size patches of skin flaking and itchiness on the face and neck, which have begun the last couple of days. I will use the Aquaphor for that. The throat seems to be pretty open and swallowing is not very difficult. The greenish phlegm is becoming less each day. Other than my concern about the facial swelling, I am doing great! Since you think the continuing facial swelling is normal, I will cancel the appointment with my PCM this afternoon.

Sorry to bother you, but I thought the face ought to be going the other direction, instead of continuing to swell after two weeks. I am ready for the healing to commence and know it should soon begin.

As always, I appreciate your time.

Your pest!

Don

-----Original Message-----
From: Pat and Bob Coonfield
Sent: Thursday, July 06, 4:05 PM
To: Don Sublett
Subject: God is great!

Don,

Pat and I rejoice with you in your recovery. I know it is not over yet, but you have come such a long way and we are thrilled for you. You guys have been in our constant thoughts and our prayers. It is so good to get the answer you want. His answers are all correct and right, but good seems better to us.

Love you and miss you, both, so very much.

In His love,

Bob and Pat

-----Original Message-----
From: Don Sublett
Sent: Thursday, July 06, 7:13 PM
To: Pat and Bob Coonfield
Subject: God is great!

Pat and Bob,

Great to hear from you! I trust all is going well with you and you are on your way back to the house, or soon will be? We look forward to seeing you!

Yes, God is great! He has certainly answered a lot of prayer over these last several weeks. It is truly remarkable how well I have done while going through treatments and I continue to be in excellent condition. My ENT doc told me last week when I showed her some facial swelling that, "You are finally acting human!" What can I say? I have just tried to be a good patient.

We do appreciate the prayers and ask that they continue. I go for a CT/PET scan on 3 Aug. and then see my ENT on the 8th. She has the OR scheduled for the 10th, just in case we need it. The obvious hope is we have killed the cancer and no surgery is required, but we will not know that until the tests are completed.

We love and miss you all, as well!

Don

IV.

The Aftermath

-----Original Message-----
From: Don Sublett
Sent: Friday, July 14, 1:10 PM
To: Support Group
Subject: Update #18

Hi Everyone!

I have received several e-mails and calls asking how I am doing, so I thought I would send out this update.

I finished treatments on 22 June and continue to do extremely well. The mouth is just about healed. I have one persistent tongue sore that I think will finally heal in another day or two, but I have been saying that for about a week now. Once that sore heals, I will begin the full transition to a normal diet, though I have eaten a few things already.

It might take a couple weeks to get to a normal diet, because of needing to get the swallowing reflex back. Small solid food bits tend to hang in the back of the throat, so it is going to take a concentrated effort to get over that. (Use of a speech therapist/pathologist has been mentioned, but I don't think we are to that juncture

169

yet.) I don't know if things hang due to throat constriction or lack of moisture. I suspect it could be a bit of both. I want to take that first big bite of hamburger or steak, but am a little hesitant to do so at the moment. Some of the taste buds on the left side of the mouth are coming back, but the right side is being slowed by the tongue sores.

The last couple of days I have only taken one dose of the Lortab pain medication a day, and that was at night. I don't know if that means there is no pain in the throat, or if I am still running on "reserve." I hope it is the former.

I go for a combined CT/PET scan on the 3rd. They will inject a radioactive sugar solution into me and the scans will register any cancers or abnormal growths which are 5mm or larger. If I read the paperwork correctly, I will know the results of the scans a couple hours after they are completed. I will follow-up with my ENT doctor on the 8th to determine a course of action based on the results from the scans. When I mentioned to my radiation oncologist during a follow-up last week that Dr. McMurphy has an operating room reserved, he said, "You won't be needing surgery!" I certainly hope his assessment is correct. However, I still have some concern about the 6mm spot which showed in the left lung on the last CT scan. The doctors seemed to think it was nothing, but it has to be of concern until proven to not be a problem. So, we continue to pray, knowing God will continue to answer those prayers.

As I look back on the events of the last three or four months, I marvel at all that has transpired—particularly, so many joining us in the battle. I also reflect on that first office visit with my ENT, when Dr. McMurphy told me of her diagnosis of cancer at the base of the tongue. At that time, she told me of the painful nature of the treatment and also said, "If you have a good support group, you will do just fine." I knew I would have a lot of support in battling the cancer, but I have to tell you, I honestly had no idea just how much support would develop, and how meaningful that support would be!

Judy and I are very thankful so many have joined and supported us in my battle with cancer. The visits, calls, cards, letters, and e-mails have all been so encouraging and uplifting. Then, to know there were literally hundreds and maybe a thousand or more praying for God to minimize the pain, and to fully heal me, is just so overwhelming. I have tried to think back to where it first really hit me that God was answering your prayers. I suspect it was when I was about half way through the treatments. What an eye-opener and faith builder that was!

The battle isn't necessarily over yet, but I can't help being encouraged about the outcome, knowing you continue to pray and that God continues to hear and answer your prayers!

We thank you from the bottom of our hearts!

Fight's On!!!

Don

Dr. McMurphy later told me she was actually concerned about where the radiation might be going, since I was not showing many signs, at all, of receiving any radiation. My skin on the jaw bones showed very little redness, minimal chafing and flaking, and there was no burning or cracking. Additionally, there was very little damage inside the mouth, or in the throat, and the mucosa remained intact.

A song came to mind, once I fully realized just how wonderfully God was answering prayers. That song was, "I Stand In Awe." There were many nights I drifted off to sleep after praying with the words of the song on my lips and in my heart. The words follow and very realistically describe our inadequacies in fully being able to describe and comprehend just how wonderful our God is.

You are beautiful beyond description,
too marvelous for words
too wonderful for comprehension,
like nothing ever seen or heard.
Who can grasp your infinite wisdom?
Who can fathom the depth of your love?
You are beautiful beyond description,
majesty enthroned above
and I stand, I stand in awe of you
and I stand, I stand in awe of you
Holy God, to whom all praise is due,
I stand in awe of you!

-----Original Message-----
From: John Fuhrmann
Sent: Friday, July 14, 5:05 PM
To: Don Sublett
Subject: Re: Update #18

Don,

Your update would be difficult to be more positive, albeit, as you said, the game is not over, but the progress is wonderful. Your entire life—and your family's—has been turned upside down, and probably will never be quite the same, but your faith and great support from so many has been a huge boost in your challenges. "Well done!" is probably the understatement of the year, but it is appropriate. Keep the faith and we will continue to watch your "six."

I attached a couple of Manitoba beauties from my time up north last week. The smiles tell the story—762 pike, lake trout, and grayling for the week—some 30 lb. pike and lakers in the mix!

Cheers and God bless

John

-----Original Message-----
From: Don Sublett
Sent: Friday, July 14, 6:31 PM
To: John Fuhrmann
Subject: Re: Update #18

John,

It has been a remarkable experience, made so much easier by the support and encouragement of so many. Cancer is not anything a person would wish to experience, but I think I am a better and more appreciative person than I was. It will be interesting to see what the future holds. As you said, our lives have been turned upside down, with maybe another twist or two before everything is said and done. I will be glad to get the CT/PET scans behind me. I feel very confident the cancer in the neck and throat is killed, but remain concerned, as mentioned, about the spot on the lung.

Those are some fabulous pictures. I bet you still have a big smile on your face! Lord willing, I'd like to try and make that trip one year if you have room to fit in an "extra." Right now, I have absolutely no muscles or stamina. I cut the grass this week over a period of three days. Of course, the humidity didn't help any, but I got it done.

Thanks for your support and prayers!

Don

-----Original Message-----
From: Herb Bruse
Sent: Friday, July 14, 6:49 PM
To: Don Sublett
Subject: Re: Update #18

Don:

Not sure I can give you any meaningful advice about your upcoming scans, but I know I have been there, as well. As best as I can remember, I took each scan with an open mind. I was not overly optimistic, nor was I expecting bad news. I was just expecting news and would deal with whatever happened.

If truth be known, I knew I was a good person, a good husband and father, had many friends who were genuinely interested in my well-being, and received a tremendous amount of strength from that knowledge. I know that may sound corny, but it worked for me. Now, fourteen years later, I feel very fortunate and look at life differently. Everyone has issues and I feel much more compassionate than I ever did before.

If you ever get a chance, read the book by Victor Frankl titled, *A Man's Search for Meaning.* Mr. Frankl was a Jewish psychiatrist who went through the German concentration camps. He has a perspective on life which makes a lot of sense to me. Perhaps you will find it useful. I have carried the book in my briefcase for over 14 years and look at it, occasionally. If you can't find it, I will send it to you.

Cheers,

Herb

-----Original Message-----
From: Don Sublett
Sent: Friday, July 14, 8:08 PM
To: Herb Bruse
Subject: Re: Update #18

Herb,

Doesn't sound corny to me at all. We all deal with things in our own way.

I don't know what the scans will or will not show, but I certainly know what I want to see. However, I expect to be prepared to deal with whatever might be revealed, and with God's help, I will do so. I, too, expect to be much more compassionate than I have been in the past, and more forthright about my faith in God and his healing power. However this plays out, I think I am a better person because of the experience. It has certainly been a wake up call!

I will order the book you reference off of Amazon and read it. I appreciate you sharing with me.

Don

-----Original Message-----
From: Roz N.
Sent: Monday, July 17, 9:43 AM
To: Don Sublett
Subject: Re: Update #18

Don,

I saw you at worship, yesterday, but didn't get to talk to you. You are looking very well. Talked to Judy and she told me how you were doing and said you couldn't wait to really eat.

At lunch, yesterday, Walt was comparing some of what he went through with how you are doing and he just couldn't believe it. We are so grateful you are doing so well. I know five years makes a difference in new medical research, but, as Christians, we know who ultimately is in control.

We will continue to pray for you and Judy, and know you are in the best hands. If we can do anything for you, please let us know.

Have a great day!

Roz

-----Original Message-----
From: Don Sublett
Sent: Monday, July 17, 4:15 PM
To: Roz N.
Subject: Re: Update #18

Roz,

I have done extremely well throughout this whole experience. I have truly been blessed through answered prayer. There is no other explanation. I know Walt had it far tougher than I have had it, probably at any point through-out. I am thankful for the research and progress made these last five years. I certainly benefited from it.

I do want to be able to eat normally again, but it is slow going. My ENT confirmed, today, that I likely still have substantial swelling in the throat, though it doesn't hurt. She tells me that even though it has been 3 ½ weeks since my last treatment, it is "still early." Knowing that, I sup-pose I can be patient a bit longer. Ha!

Sure do appreciate the continued thoughts and prayers. They mean more than you might imagine.

Don

-----Original Message-----
From: Curt Seebaldt
Sent: Wednesday, July 19, 7:38 AM
To: Don Sublett
Subject: RE: Update #18

Don,

Just got back from two weeks down in Ft. Lauderdale getting Kelly set up in his house. Not much of a vacation, unless you call scrubbing floors, painting, caulking, mowing, etc., some form of relaxation. Place looks great and he has two renters on contract. I flew back yesterday and Caron will follow with the car at the end of this week. Sounds like you are well on your way to recovery. I will buy lunch at Kinfolk's when you are ready.

Cobalt

-----Original Message-----
From: Don Sublett
Sent: Wednesday, July 19, 9:02 AM
To: Curt Seebaldt
Subject: RE: Update #18

Curt,

I was in the office, week before last, and you were out. I figured you were at the gym. Didn't realize you were down south. It sounds like things are going well for you all. We are both going to have a zero balance on vacation time!

I was supposed to follow up with my ENT doctor on 8 Aug., but that has been changed to the 11th. The OR is now set for the 15th, but she also seems to think it will not be needed. I don't know if she is keying off the radiation oncologist's opinion, or if this is her independent assessment. Regardless, I hope they are both right. If I get a clean bill of health, I will be back to work within a couple of days.

I have picked up another yeast infection in the mouth. This one is being a bit more stubborn than the first one, but I got another medicine (Nystatin) for it yesterday. Hopefully, a couple more days and it will be cleared, along with the tongue sores. I would like to get everything headed in the same direction for a change. Still unable to eat because of swelling (substantial) in the throat, so Kinfolk's (Barbeque) is on hold, but I will take you up on it as soon as I can! The doctors told me it would take six weeks to heal, so I hope to see good improvement the next two weeks. I am four weeks from my last treatment today.

Got to hit the shower. We are headed for Pensacola. Les, Dave, and Lauren are flying in at noon and Michael and his family will be in tomorrow evening. They all wanted to be here to celebrate my birthday on Sunday. I had hoped to be able to eat a hamburger with them, but will have to settle for some ice cream. Still, I suppose one shouldn't complain if all they can eat is ice cream. Ha!

Take care,

Don

-----Original Message-----
From: G. Millon Plyler
Sent: Tuesday, August 01, 8:20 PM
To: Don Sublett
Subject: Hope you are doing well

I have been praying you get good news on Thursday; stay in touch.

Millon

-----Original Message-----
From: Don Sublett
Sent: Tuesday, August 01, 9:40 PM
To: G. Millon Plyler
Subject: Hope you are doing well

Millon,

I am feeling well. Still having some minor problems in the mouth, but the taste buds are improving. The throat seems to be opening up a bit. My gag reflex is especially sensitive and that is causing a lot of the difficulty in swallowing solids. I am sure hoping that will ease before long.

I, too, am hoping for good news on Thursday, and think that is what we will get. Regardless, I will be glad to have a read on where we stand and what will have to be done if there is still cancer present.

I will let you know what we learn. The prayers are still greatly appreciated and needed.

Don

V.

THE CT/PET SCAN

-----Original Message-----
From: Don Sublett
Sent: Thursday, August 03, 2:55 PM
To: Support Group
Subject: Update

Hi Everyone,

I went today for the CT/PET scan and the results were not as good as what I was expecting or hoping for. A spot showed at the site of the primary tumor, but there were no signs of cancer anywhere else in the body. The radiologist said she is concerned cancer remains in the tongue. However, she is not certain this is the case, because the radioactive sugar can be taken up in an area because of inflammation.

The doctor said it is possible the primary tumor site is still inflamed and healing from the radiation. It is also possible there is an ulcer on the tongue or inflammation in the area for other reasons. I know I do feel some "soreness" on both sides at the back of the tongue at the moment. I don't know if this is sufficient to light up the area or not. Dr. McMurphy scoped the throat, week before last, and said everything looked good.

She also probed the tumor area of the tongue and said it felt soft. Soft, in this case, is good. So, I am not sure where we stand either.

Dr. McMurphy is presently on leave. I will see her again on the 11th to see where we go from here. At a minimum, I expect to probably have another tongue biopsy on the 15th to determine if there is actually any cancer remaining. If Dr. McMurphy opts to do the biopsy and it shows there is still cancer in the tongue, she may go ahead at that time and surgically remove it, since I believe she has the OR reserved for the entire day. I wish I had a better feel for what to expect, but I don't.

Obviously, I am a little taken aback at today's developments. It just highlights that things don't always go as you want or expect. However, we are thankful there seems to be only the one area which is cause for concern.

Clearly, the battle continues. As we press ahead to gain clarity on my condition, Judy and I ask you to continue to pray for us.

Fight's On!!!

Don

-----Original Message-----
From: Darlene Morris
Sent: Thursday, August 03, 3:54 PM
To: Don Sublett
Subject: Fight the Battle!

Yes, the battle does continue. I don't have a clue how disappointing it might feel to long for a clean scan and to not get it. Don't become discouraged! I am so sure God is in control and your positive attitude has helped immensely. Today's developments are just that—today's. Tomorrow is in His hands.

Give Judy a hug for me. How we would love to see you all. I dreamed, last night, about Germany. You are both in our prayers, Don. Thank you for the update.

In His Service,

Darlene

-----Original Message-----
From: Don Sublett
Sent: Thursday, August 03, 4:03 PM
To: Darlene Morris
Subject: Fight the Battle!

Darlene,

We would love to see you all, as well. Thoughts of Germany bring back a lot of fond memories. That was one of the best tours we ever had.

Today was disappointing, but I remain optimistic. I still have some swelling in my face and I am sure there is some in my throat, as well. It is very possible what showed up is caused by the radiation and not from cancer remaining. However, we still have to figure out exactly where we stand. I will be glad when we know for sure.

There is no doubt God is in control and that He will hear and answer our prayers. We do appreciate you continuing to bring our concerns before the Father.

Don

-----Original Message-----
From: John Fuhrmann
Sent: Thursday, August 03, 4:21 PM
To: Don Sublett
Subject: Re: Update

Prayers and hopes for good news have not, and will not, stop, Don. Easy for me to say, but nevertheless, "Keep the Faith."

Cheers

John

-----Original Message-----
From: Don Sublett
Sent: Thursday, August 03, 5:48 PM
To: John Fuhrmann
Subject: Re: Update

John,

My faith has not wavered, and will not. Also easy for me to say, but I know, ultimately, God wins.

It is very possible what showed up today is due to remaining inflammation from the radiation. They really lit me up the last two weeks and I still have swelling in the face, as well as in the throat. Still, we need to get to the bottom of this and determine if it is cancer, or not. Thus, I fully expect there will be another biopsy of the area. There may be another way to make the determination, but I don't know what it might be.

We do appreciate the continued support and prayers.

Don

****

-----Original Message-----
From: Don Sublett
Sent: Friday, August 04, 4:30 PM
To: Support Group
Subject: 4 Aug. Update

Hi again, Everyone:

Today has a bit brighter tinge than yesterday. I was so bummed this morning that I decided to call my radiation oncologist's office to see if he was available to see me and discuss the scan results. Dr. Bonanno said, "Most certainly," and asked me to stop by the radiologist to pick up a copy of the CT/PET scan, and bring it with me.

During our discussion and the exam, Dr. Bonnano noted the mouth tenderness and the facial swelling. He also palpitated the neck area and probed as far down the tongue as he could reach without deadening the throat. He, too, commented on the softness of the tongue, saying it was far different now than when I first came in for treatment. Initially, the tumor was clearly discernible when probing the tongue. Doctor Bonanno's thoughts—though he can't say with certainty—are it is a very real possibility that the radiation is still at work and that it is probably a bit early to see a clean scan in that area of the tongue. As he said, we poured a lot of radiation into the area.

Though not my primary physician, Dr. Bonnano seemed to think the approach Dr. McMurphy would take—and he would also recommend in his report to her—is to wait three or four weeks and follow up with another CT/PET scan. He said that even then, we might not see a clean scan, but would hopefully see a reduction in the uptake intensity in that area of the tongue.

He seemed to think it is too early to begin sticking needles and knives into the tongue, but said this decision rests with Dr. Mac.

I know I am not out of the woods yet, but I am relieved to learn it is not unrealistic to believe the hot spot on the scan might be caused from inflammation and not be residual cancer. Still, until scans show improvement or a biopsy is done, there is continued cause for concern.

I have to tell you that yesterday was probably my second most difficult day, in terms of emotional turmoil, since this began. The most difficult was the day I was given the initial cancer diagnosis. Judy and I *really appreciate* the outpouring of love and concern so many of you gave us yesterday. Each call and message provided tremendous encouragement.

As a good friend said yesterday, "This cancer trip is up and down all the time." There is no denying that fact, but the trip is made easier because of the love, concern, help, and prayers of our friends.

We appreciate every one of you!

Fight's On!!!

Don

-----Original Message-----
From: Linda Dwyer
Sent: Friday, August 04, 4:38 PM
To: Don Sublett
Subject: RE: 4 Aug. Update

Thank you for your update! We continue to keep you in our prayers. As I said to you last Sunday, you are probably a greater encouragement to us than we are to you, because of your strength and confidence in the Lord.

You look great!

See you soon!

Dennis, Linda, and Mandy

-----Original Message-----
From: Don Sublett
Sent: Friday, August 04, 7:25 PM
To: Linda Dwyer
Subject: RE: 4 Aug. Update

Linda,

If you only knew how much encouragement I get from notes like yours, you wouldn't be able to say that. I think we gain strength from one another, whether it is in the church building, or through e-mail. That is what makes being part of God's family so special.

Love you all!

Don

-----Original Message-----
From: G. Millon Plyler
Sent: Friday, August 04, 4:44 PM
To: Don Sublett
Subject: RE: 4 Aug. Update

Have a good weekend, and think positive. You have got cancer out of your body (except maybe one place), maybe entirely, and the radiation and chemo is done. Just trust in the Lord!
Have a good weekend, my friend.

Millon

-----Original Message-----
From: Don Sublett
Sent: Friday, August 04, 3:07 PM
To: G. Millon Plyler
Subject: RE: 4 Aug. Update

Millon,

I have been pretty positive throughout this whole experience and I know I have a lot to be thankful for. We are getting down to where the rubber meets the road—cured or not cured. That is when the realities can get to be pretty "real." I know Dr. Mac is going to be surprised at the hot spot. I don't think she even entertained the idea the cancer in the tongue would not be killed.

We will have a good weekend. We have a birthday party for the grand-daughter of a friend, this evening. That should be interesting, especially if I try to eat anything solid. I will probably spend my time running in and out of the back door. My gag reflex is super sensitive and if anything solid hits the back of the throat, it immediately grabs it and will not let it go down. So, I sit there and gag until it releases—not a pretty sight. Ha! I asked the doc, this morning, when that would ease and he told me that he didn't know. When I queried on whether it would, in fact, ease, he said, "I hope so." Probably not as much as I do. Ha!

You have a good weekend, too.

Don

Tragically, shortly after I completed treatment, Millon was killed in an automobile accident. He was a *friend* I had "known" for several years, but never met. We first became connected through a stock we each owned and discussed, periodically. We had planned to meet after I completed treatment and was up to traveling.

Millon was one of my most fierce "prayer warriors." Even though Million has passed on to his heavenly reward, I am frequently reminded of him. Millon was heavily involved with the Clemson University Tigers fan base. Probably to the point where his blood had at least a slightly orange tint. So, whenever I see or hear reference to Clemson University, I cannot help but remember Million and the fact he was one of my staunchest "prayer warriors." He is missed.

-----Original Message-----
From: Chuck S.
Sent: Friday, August 04, 4:49 PM
To: Don Sublett
Subject: Re: 4 Aug. Update

Sorry to learn things are not going as well as we had hoped they would at this point. I know you are probably feeling some anxiety about the state of your recovery, but with the continued healing process, maybe it is still a little too early for the desired results to show up? We all need to maintain a positive attitude and continue our vigilance in prayer.

Chuck

-----Original Message-----
From: Don Sublett
Sent: Friday, August 04, 3:45 PM
To: Chuck S.
Subject: Re: 4 Aug. Update

Chuck,

As you saw earlier, I got a little better slant on things today than I did yesterday. That doesn't mean there will not be some difficult times ahead.

There likely will be. Still, God is on our side and as we know, God ultimately wins.

Appreciate the thoughts and prayers.

Don

-----Original Message-----
From: Bob and Pat Coonfield
Sent: Saturday, August 05, 11:46 AM
To: Don Sublett
Subject: (no subject)

Dear Don and Judy:

Pat and I are in Bowling Green, KY, working for two weeks with the Potter Children's Home. We finally have a telephone available and are able to catch up on e-mails. Of the 50-plus messages, yours is the one we were looking for.

I would be lying to say I am overjoyed with the report, but after thinking about it a little while, I feel a lot better. God has brought us so far with this thing. I know we will beat it. It is just going to take a little longer than we'd hoped for.

Please keep us informed and know that you both continue to be in our prayers.

Love,

Bob and Pat

-----Original Message-----
From: Don Sublett
Sent: Saturday, August 05, 1:13 PM
To: Bob and Pat Coonfield
Subject: (no subject)

Pat and Bob,

Good to hear from you! I grew up in Campbellsville, KY, which is about 60 miles from Bowling Green. We just mailed a small donation to the children's home where you are a few days ago.

I, too, feel considerably better after the visit with the radiation oncologist, yesterday. I realize there are still some unknowns on my condition, but I also realize God is in control of the situation. He has been so good to me, so far. I have a difficult time accepting there is still cancer in the tongue. Yet, I realize that is certainly possible. I will be glad to see my ENT doctor on Friday and get her take on the situation. She is a sharp young doctor.

I will continue the updates when circumstances warrant and will probably provide another update on Friday, after I see her. We look forward to your return "home."

We love and appreciate you!

Don

-----Original Message-----
From: Sanford Flach
Sent: Sunday, August 06, 7:48 AM
To: Don Sublett
Subject: Re: I received the update.

Hello Don,

We received your most recent update. I try to look at it as very positive, in that the test showed no further spread of the cancer. Last year, when I completed my radiation, they waited almost three months before they would do the

PET scan, because they wanted the tongue area to have time to start healing. I had some suspicious lymph nodes at that time and they removed them. They biopsied the nodes, my tongue, and the throat, on 27 Dec. All was clear.

We will continue to keep you in our prayers and we feel confident God will heal you!

Sanford & Peggy

-----Original Message-----
From: Don Sublett
Sent: Sunday, August 06, 2:12 PM
To: Sanford Flach
Subject: Re: I received the update.

Sanford,

I, too, am glad no cancer showed in any other areas. I also appreciate knowing you waited three months before getting the PET. The receptionist at the radiation oncologist the other day told me they never do one this early, because they get a lot of false positives. The doc was a little more circumspect. I think that was because, as a general rule, one doctor will not criticize another. I am not sure why my ENT wanted one at the six week point. However, I really think (hope) my ENT is looking more at any cancerous nodes in the neck than the tongue area. That is a question I will ask on Friday.

Quite honestly, I feel like we killed the cancer in the tongue. That is why I was so surprised Thursday. God has answered an awful lot of prayer these last several months and I don't think He is done yet.

I do appreciate you sharing your experience with me, as well as your continued prayers. I will continue to keep you updated.

Don

****

-----Original Message-----
From: Don Sublett
Sent: Wednesday, August 09, 10:19 PM
To: Support Group
Subject: 9 Aug. Note

All,

I never cease to be amazed at how you can often make a (somewhat educated) guess and be wrong. I figured my radiation oncologist, Dr. Bonanno, had some good insight regarding the likely approach moving forward: too early for needles and knives; wait three or four weeks and repeat the PET scan. In fact, I think I had decided in my mind that was the way to go, and the way we would go! However, Dr. McMurphy is not buying into that. Even though Dr. McMurphy is on leave, she is obviously still involved with my case. She ordered a CT scan with contrast (dye) for me this afternoon, at Eglin. This is the same scan which revealed the tongue cancer, initially, and it is evidently not affected by inflammation, as the PET scan is. So, I went today and got the scan. I will get the results at my 8:00 A.M. appointment, on Friday. If the scan shows cancer is still present, then we will be using the OR she has reserved, on the 15th.

I am fortunate to have Dr. McMurphy as my primary doctor. She is extremely aggressive in her approach to treating my cancer and I admire her for that. While I don't relish even the slightest prospect of surgery on the tongue, there is an elementary fact which cannot be denied. The longer a cancer remains, the more it grows. The larger it grows, the more tissue which will have to be removed.

I have been asking God for clarity on the status of my cancer and it looks like He has answered another prayer.

God is good!

Fight's On!!!

Don

-----Original Message-----
From: Jon S.
Sent: Wednesday, August 09, 10:57 PM
To: Don Sublett
Subject: Re: 9 Aug. Note

Don,

Our prayers are with you, brother. Your faith is an inspiration to me. Your comments have made it like we have been going through this with you. Through the peaks and valleys, your faith has never wavered. From someone who still struggles with how amazing God is, your story and faith has allowed my own faith and belief in God to mature. Thank you for sharing your story with all of us, and thank you for your witness in these hard times.

To God be the Glory,

Jon

-----Original Message-----
From: Don Sublett
Sent: Thursday, August 10, 5:08 PM
To: Jon S.
Subject: Re: 9 Aug. Note

Jon,

Thank you for the very kind words. I appreciate the opportunity to share my experience. My faith, too, has grown much stronger as I realized just how involved God is in my progress. He is truly amazing.

Don

-----Original Message-----
From: Paula Willcox
Sent: Thursday, August 10, 6:15 AM
To: Don Sublett
Subject: Re: 9 Aug. Note

Do you consider the possibility the CT scan will *not* show cancer, and therefore, the OR not be needed? I do, and will, pray that way, dear friend. This time of not knowing is awful and scary. Our hearts are with you, and we love you.

Paula

-----Original Message-----
From: Don Sublett
Sent: Thursday, August 10, 8:53 AM
To: Paula Willcox
Subject: Re: 9 Aug. Note

Paula,

I certainly have considered the scan will show no cancer and I also think that is very likely. However, I think it wise to try and prepare for as many eventualities as you can. We are getting down to the point where we will know what is ahead. While that is good, it is also cause for a bit of apprehension, which is probably just normal human reaction. My faith is not wavering. God will see us through. I have no doubt in that, because He is hearing our prayers.

We love you and Ray, too!

Don

****

-----Original Message-----
From: Don Sublett
Sent: Thursday, August 10, 10:13 AM
To: Support Group
Subject: 9 Aug. Note... Addendum

Everyone,

I sense from reading some responses to my earlier note that some think I am focused on the negative aspects of tomorrow's appointment more than the positive. I don't believe that is the case at all. I believe there is a very distinct probability that yesterday's scan will *not* show any cancer, but to not acknowledge otherwise would not be realistic. If there is one thing I have tried to be throughout this entire experience, it has been *realistic*.

We saw some amazing results in the way the cancerous nodes in the neck responded to the chemo and radiation. Those two nodes were each about one-inch in diameter—about the same size as the cancer on the tongue—and they just "melted" away. Other than last week's CT/PET scan results (which could have been due to inflammation, of which I certainly have a lot remaining), there is no reason to not believe the cancer in the tongue responded in the same way, even though there was considerably more tissue and bone the radiation had to penetrate in order to kill the cancer. Yet, believing is one thing and knowing is another. Ultimately, I have to know one way or the other, and I can't help but be a bit apprehensive as the proverbial "moment of truth" approaches.

I approach tomorrow's appointment with guarded optimism, but still fully realizing there might be some additional difficult times ahead. If there are, I know God will be right there with me, just as He has been from the beginning of this experience, and throughout to this moment.

I will let you know, tomorrow, what we learn.

Fight's On!!!

Don

-----Original Message-----
From: Glenn G.
Sent: Thursday, August 10, 10:33 AM
To: Don Sublett
Subject: RE: 9 Aug. Note... Addendum

I think your attitude is exactly where it should be. You have to be realistic with these issues. God is in control, but that doesn't mean he will give us the answer we want. Anticipating the best, but preparing for the worst, is not a lack of faith. It is only prudent, given the circumstances. Your attitude and focus throughout this ordeal has been an inspiration to a lot of people, me included. Hang in there and let us know about tomorrow.

Love you, brother.

Glenn

-----Original Message-----
From: Don Sublett
Sent: Thursday, August 10, 10:35 AM
To: Glenn G.
Subject: RE: 9 Aug. Note… Addendum

Glenn,

That was what I was trying to express to folks. You just can't stick your head in the sand and trudge on.

Love you all, too!

Don

-----Original Message-----
From: Ann W.
Sent: Thursday, August 10, 10:51 AM
To: Don Sublett
Subject: Re: 9 Aug. Note… Addendum

Uncle Don,

You are the one who is amazing. Your strength and approach to this difficult situation show each and every one of your friends and family what a truly special person you are. I am proud to be part of your family! All of us hold a new respect for our faith because of you. With that said, you are in my thoughts and prayers. I am sure, whatever the results, God will make sure it is what you can handle.

Love always,

Ann

God grant me the serenity to accept the things I cannot change, courage to change the things I can, and the wisdom to know the difference.

-----Original Message-----
From: Don Sublett
Sent: Thursday, August 10, 11:01 AM
To: Ann W.
Subject: Re: 9 Aug. Note... Addendum

Ann,

There has been an awful lot of answered prayer as treatment for my cancer has unfolded. Once I realized just how much God is involved, it made dealing with the cancer just that much easier. My faith has been strengthened tremendously, as well.

It will be good to learn the status of things, tomorrow. I appreciate the thoughts and prayers.

Judy and I love you, too.

Don

-----Original Message-----
From: Denise G.
Sent: Thursday, August 10, 11:04 AM
To: Don Sublett
Subject: Re: 9 Aug. Note... Addendum

I felt your Aug. 9th update was very positive. I am so glad you have taken an active role in your own care and that you have a doctor bold enough to be right on top of your care. It is obvious to me that your faith in God is at an all-time high. Keep on with the fight as you have been. I commend you and Judy. How is she?

I have not been through cancer, but have had health problems since I was a child—some not so serious, and some very serious. Today, my health is still not good. Your writings have given me the courage and insight to be more proactive in my own health care with the physicians. Keep up the good fight, with the Lord by your side.

In Christian Love,

Denise

-----Original Message-----
From: Don Sublett
Sent: Thursday, August 10, 4:24 PM
To: Denise G.
Subject: Re: 9 Aug. Note... Addendum

Denise,

I am very fortunate to have a doctor who is so aggressive and also willing to use the resources at her disposal. I am optimistic about the outcome, regardless of whether we are done with actions to kill the cancer or not. Obviously,

I hope surgery is not in the works, but I am glad we still have that as an option. Some are not as fortunate.

Our health is very precious to us. Sometimes we don't fully realize that until it is threatened. That threat makes us more aware of God and his presence in our life.

I appreciate knowing that sharing this experience has been helpful to you. It has also been helpful to me in sorting things out and forcing me to look at things with open eyes. Those open eyes have helped me to see God at work throughout this experience. He does answer prayer.

Judy is well and is back in the Rocky Bayou school classroom.

I hope your health improves. Being sick is not fun, especially when you don't feel sick.

We appreciate the love and prayers.

Don

VI.

HEADED FOR SURGERY

-----Original Message-----
From: Don Sublett
Sent: Friday, August 11, 12:54 PM
To: Support Group
Subject: 11 Aug. Update

Hi All,

I am headed for the OR Tuesday for a lymph node dissection on the right side. This was pretty much the proverbial "bolt out of the blue." In contrast to what the Radiologist told us last Thursday, it turns out there are two suspicious nodes, about 7mm in size, remaining. The procedure will last five to six hours, due to the meticulous/tedious nature of it. We need to pray for steady hands.

Dr. McMurphy said I would probably have more pain from the biopsy than from the neck dissection. My guess is the pain might be there, but I don't plan on feeling it. A drain will be placed in the neck and I will go home when there is less than 30cc drainage in a 24-hour period. I can expect to be hospitalized for at least two nights.

Prior to starting the neck dissection, Dr. McMurphy will do a tongue biopsy and send it to the pathologist for study. However, she assured us we will not get the results immediately. The tissue sample will most likely be sent to the Air Force Institute of Pathology and it will take two or three weeks for the results. Due to the fact it is radiated tissue, it will look funky and we still may not know from the biopsy if there is cancer remaining in the tongue. If that is the case, there will be additional CT/PET scans, followed by another biopsy. In spite of what we learn (or don't learn) from the scans, tissue samples will be the final determinant on whether or not cancer remains in the tongue. Dr. McMurphy will not rely entirely on scans.

I don't know what the CT scan from Wednesday showed on the tongue. I failed to ask, because we spent so much time discussing the surprise dissection. I will follow up with her on that, but evidently not much was to be gleaned.

Dr. McMurphy talked about surgery to the tongue in case it comes to that. In her words, "Tongue surgery is a morbid procedure." Entry would be from the left side of the neck. They would carve out the cancerous tissue and replace it with tissue from the thigh. A trachea would also be required. I suppose until healing took place, or the swelling went down enough to permit normal breathing. Chewing, swallowing, and speech would have to be relearned, and speech would likely be severely (my interpretation) compromised, but I would still be able to make myself understood—not a pretty picture, nor is it a road anyone would want to travel. However, it can't be ruled out at this time.

The up and down nature of this experience continues. I firmly believe God is not going to put more on my plate than I can handle, but I do sense I am being "stretched" a bit. Still, there is the realization that I am not alone in fighting the cancer. Judy and I continue to solicit your prayers.

Fight's On!!!

Don

Judy and I were sitting in the waiting room with Paula and Ray the morning of the appointment, when Dr. McMurphy came out to the receptionist's desk. She and the receptionist were discussing the location of surgery for some of her patients. (Eglin AFB has an arrangement with Fort Walton Beach Medical Center where base surgeons will use the medical center's OR, at times.) Dr. McMurphy told the receptionist that another of her patients would be going to Fort Walton Beach for surgery, and while looking at me, said, "Mr. Sublett's surgery will be here."

Ray had been talking to Paula and he missed the exchange between Dr. McMurphy and the receptionist, so I leaned over and told him it looked like I was headed for surgery. Since the radiologist had told me the only hot spot was on the tongue, I assumed it was tongue surgery. That prospect was very disappointing. Even though I was surprised at the fact surgery was looming, I was *very much heartened* when I learned major surgery to the tongue was not imminent.

-----Original Message-----
From: Steve F.
Sent: Friday, August 11, 1:03 PM
To: Don Sublett
Subject: RE: 11 Aug. Update

Don,

I know I haven't sent any replies to your previous updates, but I want you to know you are in my prayers every night, at home. Last night,

I added you to my Knights of Columbus Prayer Chain, at our business meeting. Keep up the spirits and you will make it through this trial.

Fuzzy

-----Original Message-----
From: Don Sublett
Sent: Friday, August 11, 1:24 PM
To: Steve F.
Subject: RE: 11 Aug. Update

Fuz,

I appreciate that. In spite of all the turmoil and uncertainty, I know the prayers are being answered. What's that old saying? Something about, "I have miles and miles to go before I sleep." Looks like I have got another mile or two to travel.

Don

-----Original Message-----
From: Marilyn Jones
Sent: Friday, August 11, 2:28 PM
To: Don Sublett
Subject: Re: Update - 11 Aug.

Dear Don,

I will continue praying through Tuesday, and in fact, through the coming weeks. This is a tough blow for you. I hope you will get the best possible care and be able to overcome this continuing adversity.

What a great example you are for your brothers and sisters.

Love,

Marilyn

-----Original Message-----
From: Don Sublett
Sent: Friday, August 11, 3:35 PM
To: Marilyn Jones
Subject: Re: Update - 11 Aug.

Marilyn,

This did come as a surprise. I thought we were clear of this hurdle, but I guess we got the "big picture" Thursday afternoon. When the doctor went to write her report, she must have drilled down into the scan and saw the nodes. It would have been nice if she had passed along the info.

We do appreciate the continued prayers. In spite of the way things are occurring, I am certain God continues to hear and answer our prayers.

Don

-----Original Message-----
From: Judy Merrill
Sent: Friday, August 11, 3:17 PM
To: Don Sublett
Subject: Re: Update - 11 Aug.

Dear Don and Judy,

I cannot imagine what all you both are going through. This has been a really tough road and it does not look like the road is any better, soon, for you. Please know you are loved and my prayers, along with many others, are for you. Take each day as it comes and leave the rest to our Lord.

Thanks for keeping us updated.

Love through Christ,

Judy

-----Original Message-----
From: Don Sublett
Sent: Friday, August 11, 4:38 PM
To: Judy Merrill.
Subject: Re: Update - 11 Aug.

Judy,

This is a real surprise to us because we were told there was nothing to be concerned about other than the area on the tongue. So, this came at us out of left field. I know lymph node dissection is pretty normal when dealing with this cancer and it would have no doubt been easier on us if there had been an indication it would be required. Since it is required, we will deal with it and move on. My sincere hope is the cancer in the tongue is dead. That is the surgery I do not want to have to deal with. The after-effects are significant.

We do appreciate the concern and prayers. I am glad we have God and our friends on our side. I can't imagine what it would be like if we didn't.

In Christ,

Don

-----Original Message-----
From: Penny Bagwell
Sent: Friday, August 11, 3:22 PM
To: Don Sublett
Subject: Prayers are with you.

Hang in there, brother Don. Amazing, positive techniques and procedures are available that we didn't have even five years ago. Sounds like you have a great bunch of doctors who see you as a person and not as a number. You guys keep thinking positive thoughts and we will keep you in our prayers, for your healing and strength to face what is to come. Don't hesitate to ask if you need us in any way, from yard work to lending a shoulder to lean on.

God Bless,

Penny

-----Original Message-----
From: Penny Bagwell
Sent: Friday, August 11, 4:43 PM
To: Don Sublett
Subject: Prayers are with you.

Penny,

I am fortunate to have a superb medical team which has my best interests at heart. They are young, capable, and aggressive. Both of the ENTs which will be involved in my surgery trained at MD Anderson, over in Houston, and are up-to-date.

I am optimistic about the outcome of all this, but am hopeful we can get beyond the stage where surprises keep popping up. Everyone I know of who has had this cancer has had the lymph node dissection, as well. I thought I was going to be different, but I see that I am not. They all have, also, had the cancer in the tongue killed. So, I certainly hope I am like them in that regard, as well.

We *do* appreciate the offers of help and the shoulder to lean on. We are not bashful folks, so we will not hesitate to call. More than that, though, we appreciate the prayers. I know God is deeply involved here and am thankful for that!

Love you all,

Don

-----Original Message-----
From: Sanford Flach
Sent: Friday, August 11, 9:14 PM
To: Don Sublett
Subject: Re: I received the update.

Hi Don,

I just read your latest update and it sounds like you are scheduled for the same, or similar, surgery I had for the removal of two nodes. I was told they were still suspicious after my radiation and chemo, so they were removing them as a precaution. The surgery was very simple and they installed a drain as you described. I spent the afternoon and evening in the recovery room and was moved to ICU late that night. The following day, I was sent home. We are hoping and praying your procedure will turn out to be as simple as mine was. I was programmed with all the other dreaded things which could have been, but we just kept praying God would heal me.

I just went to my ENT today and he said everything looked great, after viewing my throat with his fiber-optic light/scope. I guess I should know the name of that thing by now, as he uses it on me every month. He told me he would schedule me for another PET scan, in November. He said he saw a lot of radiation scarring, but that was normal after the regimen I was put through. He saw no signs of cancer.

Peggy forwarded your latest update to our preacher and asked him to put you on our church prayer list. We will certainly keep you in our prayers!

Sanford & Peggy

-----Original Message-----
From: Don Sublett
Sent: Friday, August 11, 10:41 PM
To: Sanford Flach
Subject: Re: I received the update.

Sanford and Peggy,

I appreciate the info. I am not too concerned about the procedure on Tuesday, but certainly don't relish having to go through it. It does come as a real surprise, because the radiologist told us last Thursday there were no signs of cancer, other than, perhaps, on the tongue.

I am glad things continue to go well with your follow-on care. That has to be a big relief to you. I certainly hope this is the last surgery I have to undergo, other than maybe a biopsy or two, and that we don't progress to the point where they have to actually cut on the tongue.

I am still primarily on the feeding tube. The gag reflex is hyper-sensitive. If anything solid hits the back of the throat, it hangs. I can take liquids and smooth, creamy foods, but no solids yet. I am told it is due to inflammation in the throat. I also still have swelling in the face, tenderness in the mouth, and the swelling in the throat. I am hoping all of this eases soon. The guy I go to church with wasn't able to eat solid foods for over nine weeks, after his last radiation treatment. He and I both used the feeding tube. Did you experience anything like this?

I also appreciate that you have put me on your church's prayer list. Some might look at what is going on and say God is not at work here. I would have to respectfully disagree. I know God continues to hear and answer prayer.

Thanks again, Sanford.

Don

-----Original Message-----
From: Sanford Flach
Sent: Saturday, August 12, 4:11 PM
To: Don Sublett
Subject: Re: I received the update.

Hi Don,

I did not ever get a feeding tube, although I very much wanted one toward the end of my radiation. By that time, they said I had done so well without it that it would be best to tough it out a little longer and they raised my pain patch strength to 100mg. Did they ever put you on the pain patch? I can't remember the name of the patch. I started out at 25mg and soon went to 50mg, and then 75mg, and ultimately, to 100mg. They also gave me a morphine elixir. I guess looking back, now, at the fact that I kept my swallowing mechanism active enough to swallow some smooth, and a little not-so-smooth foods, was in the long run, beneficial to me. Within a few weeks after I finished radiation, my swallowing started to improve and I started working my way down the drug chain to where I was eventually off all pain drugs. I still have some difficulty swallowing and will probably always have that problem. The only medication I take now is my blood pressure pill, a few vitamins, and a baby aspirin.

Hang in there, as each passing day will bring you better health and less pain.

Sanford

-----Original Message-----
From: Don Sublett
Sent: Saturday, August 12, 5:39 PM
To: Sanford Flach
Subject: Re: I received the update.

Sanford,

Thanks, once again, for the insight. The guy I go to church with still has difficulty swallowing, after more than five years—particularly, he says, steak, hamburger, and bread. Walt also has a separation around his esophagus, which causes occasional problems in swallowing. He told me his last treatment was on 1 May and that he choked down a hot dog on July 4th. Said it about killed him and he got sicker than a dog, but he did it. I am seven weeks past my last treatment, so I may have another couple weeks, or so, before the gag reflex eases much more. I was able to gargle yesterday for the first time. Previously, every time I gargled, I would gag something horrible. So, I am glad to see that small amount of improvement.

I understand from a nurse at church that they have "marijuana in a pill," which can relax the gag reflex. Her mother received it when she was going through chemo. I don't want to have to go that route and am hopeful that, with a little more time, I can make the transition to a solid diet and get rid of the feeding tube.

I was given patches of Fentanyl near the end of my treatment, when I thought things were really going to heat up on me. However, I never had to use them. I stayed on the Lortab, throughout, and was comfortable with it. I know God had to have had a hand in my pain management, but I also think having my eleven day break in the middle allowed me to heal some. Thus, maybe taking the ultimate edge off of the pain. I also got the Intensity Modulated Radiation Treatment (IMRT), which is the "targeted" radiation, at eight different points in the head, neck, and upper chest, where the lymph nodes are.

Even though I still have some discomfort, as I described above, I wouldn't really call it pain. It is more of a nuisance than anything. I am very fortunate.

Thanks again for sharing your experience with me. It is very helpful knowing some of the things you also experienced. I will let you know how I fare after the surgery, later this week.

Don

-----Original Message-----
From: Billy N.
Sent: Saturday, August 12, 8:39 PM
To: Don Sublett
Subject: Re: Update - 11 Aug.

Mr. Sublett,

I pray to God every day to give me strength and wisdom, because those are two things I know I lack. I have known you for years. However, I don't know you very well, but your face is the face I see in my mind when I pray and picture the kind of person into which I hope God will one day mold me. Your faith in the Lord through your current ordeal is continuing to inspire me to become the person I know I need to be. I have a hard time expressing myself sometimes, but please know Rowena and I both care about you and Mrs. Sublett very much, and both of you are constantly in our prayers. Thank you for your updates; you may never know what your words mean in someone else's life, but God is working through you.

God is good,

Billy

-----Original Message-----
From: Don Sublett
Sent: Saturday, August 12, 9:51 PM
To: Billy N.
Subject: Re: Update - 11 Aug.

Billy,

I am touched deeply by your compliment. I know God is real and that he works in our lives in various ways. This experience has also increased my faith, because I have seen and felt God at work in handling the effects from the treatments for my cancer. I know that will continue.

We love you and your family tremendously, and most certainly appreciate the prayers you offer on our behalf!

Don

-----Original Message-----
From: Jerry McCormick
Sent: Sunday, August 13, 2:32 PM
To: Don Sublett
Subject: Re: Update - 11 Aug.

Bro. Don,

Thanks for including me & Janet in your e-mail group. We have been receiving your e-mails concerning your health issues and have been uplifted by your faith. Truly, there is a "peace that surpasses all understanding" we, as Christians, enjoy.

I stand amazed at how knowledgeable you are concerning your personal health issues. I was oblivious concerning my heart bypass operation. I depended upon Janet to just take care of me and to deal with the details. She continues to do the same for me, even in giving me my "pills." I couldn't tell you the specifics on any of them. I thank God for her for many reasons.

I sense you have gone through a lot of pain and stress during this time period. I commend you on your bright outlook and your trust in God. We wanted to come see you on a recent visit to Niceville, but Judy had shingles and we were told it was not wise. We would like to visit you when we drop down to Niceville on our next trip, if it is ok and convenient with you guys.

You have been put into a unique position to give your "witness" as far as what God has done for you. I am proud of the way you are handling your difficult situation.

We would be happy to do anything for you that we can, and we continue to pray for you.

Love in Christ,

Jerry & Janet

-----Original Message-----
From: Don Sublett
Sent: Monday, August 14, 2:27 PM
To: Jerry McCormick
Subject: Re: Update - 11 Aug.

Jerry,

So many folks have told me they are encouraged by my e-mails. I am sure they could not be any more encouraged than I am by the responses I get. I am really uplifted by the fact so many are praying for me. It means more than I can adequately express.

I really haven't gone through much pain at all. I was "comfortable" on the Lortab and never had to progress to stronger pain meds. I am thankful for that. Even now, I am in no pain. There is some roughness in the back of the throat and tongue, but it is more like a sore throat than anything else. However, I do think the stress level has risen significantly. I was asked to lead prayer in Bible Class this morning and to include myself. I made it through just fine, until I got to myself and I sort of fell apart. I didn't realize things were so "tight" inside, but evidently they are. Still, I will be glad to have the surgery behind me on Tuesday.

Judy did have a nice case of shingles a few weeks back, but is recovered from them, now. She has had them before, but this was nearly the "mother of all cases," I think. You are welcome to visit us anytime. We would love to see you all.

Don

****

-----Original Message-----
From: Don Sublett
Sent: Monday, August 14, 3:52 PM
To: Support Group
Subject: Info on Tomorrow

All,

I have a report time, tomorrow, of 6:00 A.M. for an 8:00 A.M. surgery. I will report to the 2nd floor surgical unit. Some have told me they plan to be there and wait with Judy and Michael. We are certainly grateful for the support, as waiting is always one of the hardest parts. The waiting area for friends and family is on the *fourth* floor.

Your prayers are still very much appreciated.

The fight's still on!

Don

-----Original Message-----
From: Billy T.
Sent: Monday, August 14, 4:02 PM
To: Don Sublett
Subject: RE: Info on Tomorrow

Don:

I have been thinking and praying for you and Judy. I told my Sunday morning Bible Class about your situation and we have prayed for you as a class. I am sure other individuals have done the same. Many in the class remember the Sublett family.

I have used you as an example several times, in the class, as one who has strong faith and reliance on God.

Soldier on!

Billy T.

-----Original Message-----
From: Don Sublett
Sent: Monday, August 14, 5:35 PM
To: Billy T.
Subject: RE: Info on Tomorrow

Billy,

Judy and I most certainly appreciate the thoughts and prayers of so many. I know God continues to hear and answer our prayers. Some folks might look at me having to have surgery and think that God is not involved. I would have to respectfully disagree.

Judy and I are tremendously comforted and blessed by our friends, and our God, as we fight this cancer. We hope to be able to come over to Palo Alto before long and personally thank the family for their prayers and support.

I will continue to soldier on, just as I have!

Don

-----Original Message-----
From: Jane Keller
Sent: Monday, August 14, 4:04 PM
To: Don Sublett
Subject: RE: Info on Tomorrow

So glad Michael is there and that your support team will also be there with Judy. Prayers are going up all over the U.S.! Joe sends his love from New York. Onward Christian soldier!

Love to all,

Jane

-----Original Message-----
From: Don Sublett
Sent: Monday, August 14, 5:39 PM
To: Jane Keller
Subject: RE: Info on Tomorrow

Jane,

We do have a tremendous amount of support in so many ways. It really makes us realize just how blessed we are. This soldier is soldiering on and is ready to get this behind him.

We love you all!

Don

I received many very meaningful communications while I was going through treatment, but the note and stone from Carole Long was very unique. Carole wrote:

Dear Don,

Topper and I have appreciated your e-mail updates so much. You have been in our prayers daily and we are so thankful for your progress, and your healing.

I know Topper told you about my prayers (at the Wailing Wall) for you, while I was in Israel. I also assume he mentioned the stone I am enclosing.

The stone was picked up from the stream bed in the Valley of Elah, where David gathered his stones to slay Goliath. Several of my traveling companions have had some trying times since returning home and have used the stone to hold onto, and remind them of, I Samuel 17:47, "the battle is the Lord's..." and also Psalm 95:1 "Jesus is the Rock of our salvation."

Anyway, I wanted to share the stone with you. It is small, but is thought to be about the size David used to kill the giant. The letters on the stone are in the old Hebrew and spell DAVID. Our Israeli guide wrote the name on the stones for us.

We look forward to future updates and to seeing you when we return to Destin.

Give Judy my love and regards.

Love,

Carole

I have carried the stone Carole sent every day since I received it. A couple of times when going through the TSA checkpoint at an airport an agent has seen the rock and commented, "I see you have a lucky rock." My reply is, "That is my reminder rock. It serves to remind me that the battle belongs to the Lord and that Jesus is the rock of our salvation." Each time I received a nod of concurrence.

The rock is indeed an unusual reminder of just how blessed we are.

-----Original Message-----
From: Skip Morgan.
Sent: Monday, August 14, 10:16 AM
To: Don Sublett
Subject: Prayers

Dear Don,

You are in my prayers. I cannot begin to know what you are going through! All I have known, all my life, has been a very hard time. You can be sure to know it! Sometimes we are not delivered from the fiery furnace, but into it. God has promised to *conform* you to the image of his son—not always a happy life. Through much suffering *was Jesus* made *perfect*!

God has been working on me very hard for a long time. I must be a real hardhead, but I would change nothing if I could start life all over again. To be saved from sin is an incredible experience, but to be saved from myself makes me whole and complete. I tried, for years, to live the Christian life, but about 22 years ago He made it real to me that I could not. The normal Christian life is Jesus Christ, living *His* life through you. Trust him, Don.

Love,

Skip

-----Original Message-----
From: Don Sublett
Sent: Monday, August 14, 2:14 PM
To: Skip Morgan
Subject: Prayers

Skip,

Good to hear from you again, especially on the eve of my surgery.

Probably the toughest thing I am going through, and have gone through for a while, now, is all the uncertainty. This surgery is a complete surprise and we haven't been, and probably will not be, able to nail down whether the cancer is killed for a while. If it was somewhere else in the body, other than the tongue, we could likely say, "Let's go cut it out." The fact it came up in the tongue puts things in a different perspective. That is an area you don't relish cutting into. I am optimistic we will not need to, because they poured a tremendous amount of radiation into it. Still, I obviously can't say for sure one way or the other.

What I can say, though, is God has seen me through to this point and I am sure He will bring me through the rest of the way. I have complete confidence and trust in Him. As mentioned previously to some others, you have to wonder how people without faith, or with a weak faith, make it through something like what I have been experiencing, or what you have experienced for many years, now. You and I both know how great it is to have Christ in our lives! For that, we can be very thankful.

Love you, too, Skip!

Don

-----Original Message-----
From: Donna A.
Sent: Monday, August 14, 4:24 PM
To: Don Sublett
Subject: RE: Info on tomorrow.

Don,

Dear brother, please know our love, thoughts, and prayers are with you, Judy, Michael, Leslie, and their families. You are right; waiting is one of the hardest parts. We are there with you in spirit, Don. God and His angels are watching over and taking care of you. Angels may sound kinda funny, but I believe we all have angels watching over us at these times. May God bless you with his presence, peace, and comfort. We love you and Judy dearly.

Love In Him,

Donna A.

-----Original Message-----
From: Don Sublett
Sent: Monday, August 14, 5:01 PM
To: Donna A.
Subject: RE: Info on tomorrow.

Donna,

I know there are angels which God uses. We do appreciate the thoughts and prayers so very much.

Love you all!

Don

-----Original Message-----
From: Dave and Leslie Miller
Sent: Monday, August 14, 6:39 PM
To: Don Sublett
Subject: Re: Info on tomorrow.

Dad,

I have heard from many friends today and they all want you to know they are praying for you, and the medical staff which will be involved tomorrow. I am looking forward to hearing a good report tomorrow afternoon. Keep fighting!

Love,

Leslie

-----Original Message-----
From: Dave and Leslie Miller
Sent: Monday, August 14, 5:01 PM 8:08 PM
To: Don Sublett
Subject: Re: Info on tomorrow.

Les,

Let everyone know we appreciate the prayers and support.

Love you,

Dad

-----Original Message-----
From: Robert Cannon
Sent: Tuesday, August 15, 10:56 AM
To: Don Sublett
Subject: Update

Hi, Don:

Darlene Morris has been keeping us updated by forwarding your e-mails. You have been in our prayers and will continue in them as long as needed. In thinking about your belief that God will not allow us to have more than we can handle, I have often thought He has a *lot* more confidence in me than I have in myself and have often wished He'd set the bar a little lower. It hasn't ever worked that way, though, so I just have to trust in His judgment.

Hang in there!

Bob

-----Original Message-----
From: Don Sublett
Sent: Tuesday, August 15, 11:18 AM
To: Robert Cannon
Subject: Update

Bob,

I am pretty sure God knows us better than we know ourselves. I know my faith has grown through this experience. There have been some ups and downs, but He has been the one constant. I am amazed at how well I have been able to hold up physically and mentally.
We are really blessed.

Don

****

-----Original Message-----
From: Don Sublett
Sent: Tuesday, August 15, 4:49 PM
To: Support Group
Subject: 15 Aug. Status

Hi All,

This is Michael, filling in for my father. Dad made it through surgery today without a hitch. He is resting in his room as I am typing this. What was supposed to have been six hours was more along the lines of four to five. We received a call in the waiting room at about 1:00 P.M., letting us know they were closing him up. We were all quite surprised, as the last we had heard it would take a minimum of six hours. The doctor said he cooperated nicely. Therefore, it didn't take as long.

Now, for the real news. The doctor did the biopsy first. She said the tongue felt soft and she felt confident the biopsy would come back negative for cancer. She informed us dad has a jugular vein the size of a large carrot and steered clear of it. They removed two lymph nodes without a problem. He experienced some nausea after the surgery was completed. As I said earlier, he is resting now.

We thank everyone who came by, today, to sit with us. It sure is nice to have friends like you all. Please keep the prayers coming as we are not completely out of the woods yet.

Love,

Michael and Judy

****

-----Original Message-----
From: Don Sublett
Sent: Thursday, August 17, 1:44 PM
To: Support Group
Subject: 17 Aug. Update... I am Home

Hi Folks!

I am home and I am a mess. According to Dr. McMurphy, my incision looks great, though!

I figured I would have gauze wrapped around my neck and maybe look like a mummy coming out of surgery, but the incision is covered by ¾" steri-strips instead. There is numbness in the right side of the neck and a fair amount of swelling. She took one drain out of the neck this morning, but I still have another literally hanging out of my neck, secured by a stitch. It will help keep the swelling down. This drain will come out either tomorrow or Monday. It depends on whether there is less than 30cc drainage in 24-hours. My guess is Monday. I have a droopy lip on the right side, which will eventually right itself, but it could take three months. Some folks might think that an improvement to my looks! Dr. McMurphy mentioned prior to the surgery that there might be some impact on the elevator muscle in the right shoulder and she was correct. It is a little stiff because of the nerve being messed with. She assured me three or four times that both she and Dr. Moore, ENT Chief and her office surgeon/partner, left all four of the nerves intact. There will be some recovery time involved.

I probably will not be cleared to go back to work before the end of September. I sense she was a bit assertive with my CIGNA insurance Short Term Disability case manager yesterday. Dr.

Mac feels pretty certain we will know by then if any additional procedures will be required. She is optimistic going forward and I can assure you she got enough tongue tissue to enable a diagnosis on the biopsy, if it is doable, from the condition of the radiated tissue.

She checked on me three times, yesterday, and we discussed some other aspects of my case, just so I have a better understanding of some things that have transpired. My throat is pretty raw and one reason for that is I was intubated twice, on Tuesday. Once with a small tube, so she could have room to do the biopsy, and a second time because the first tube was too small to keep air in the lungs. She spent some time examining the tongue and throat before the lymph node dissection.

I finally got her to tell me how long it might take to transition to a normal diet, because my gag reflex is hyper-sensitive and there is still an awful lot of swelling in the throat. She said it could take as long as six months. At least I know what is going on is normal for the condition the throat is in.

Dr. Mac was just as impressed with the support so many of you provided Tuesday and Wednesday, as Judy, Michael, and I are appreciative. I know Judy and Michael appreciated having the company while I was in surgery and I certainly appreciate the fact so many came out to lend that physical support. I also appreciate the visits—even if I was barely there for a few of them, especially Tuesday afternoon. I think I overdid it a little bit yesterday, too, but that is okay.

One of the first things Dr. Mac asked me when my case was just beginning was if I had a good support group. She saw first-hand the last couple of days just how great you are and what she physically saw was only the tip of the iceberg. I also think she felt the prayer which has been offered this week. I know I have, and I also know she appreciated being able to join those in the waiting room at the Eglin Hospital in prayer when she came out to let everyone know how the surgery went. She was touched by your faith and the support you provided Judy and Michael.

As Michael said in his note to you, we are still not fully out of the woods. However, I know without a doubt God continues to bless us each step of the way. For that, I am extremely grateful to Him, as well as to you for the concern, support, and love.

We are tremendously blessed!

Fight's On!!!

Don

One of the most remarkable aspects of my cancer treatment is the relationship with Dr. McMurphy. As you have seen, I had access to her at any time, via e-mail. Then, as Dr. McMurphy cleared me to leave the hospital, she started to give me her pager number, but said she didn't really like the pager because she sometimes didn't get her pages when inside the hospital, so she gave me her cell phone number, as well. Dr. McMurphy said she and Dr. Moore had begun doing things differently, since they arrived. I certainly must agree that they have, indeed! I never had to use the phone number, but it was good to have it, in case it was needed.

I always tried to be very judicious in approaching Dr. McMurphy through e-mail, realizing I was not her only patient. To her credit, Dr. McMurphy always replied.

-----Original Message-----
From: Stan N.
Sent: Thursday, August 17, 1:55 PM
To: Don Sublett
Subject: RE: 17 Aug. Update... I am Home

That is good to hear. Glad you are feeling a little better and you are able to share your feelings extremely well. I hesitated to ask her (Dr. McMurphy) to join us in prayer, but she said something about praying for you, so I thought what is the worst she can say if we invited her to join us? She seems like a very caring doctor and I think you are in very good hands. God bless, and stay on the recovering road you seem to be on.

Stan

-----Original Message-----
From: Don Sublett
Sent: Thursday, August 17, 1:59 PM
To: Stan N.
Subject: RE: 17 Aug. Update... I am Home

Thanks, Stan.

It would be impossible to find better care than what she has given us. Appreciate you being there yesterday.

Don

-----Original Message-----
From: Lee G.
Sent: Thursday, August 17, 6:58 PM
To: Don Sublett
Subject: RE: 17 Aug. Update... I am Home

Don,

You are a tough old bird; already home? Glad to hear it. Doc have any words on how the removed lymph nodes looked?

Will keep praying,

Lee Gay

-----Original Message-----
From: Don Sublett
Sent: Thursday, August 17, 8:04 PM
To: Lee G.
Subject: RE: 17 Aug. Update... I am Home

Lee,

I don't know how tough I am, but having good surgeons is sure nice. She is optimistic there was no cancer in the nodes and it seems, also, the tongue. She didn't tell me that directly. I will be glad to get the biopsy results back to confirm her thoughts, but I have to try and keep my equilibrium until then.
God keeps answering prayer, so we will just keep on praying.

Don

-----Original Message-----
From: Lee G.
Sent: Thursday, August 17, 7:32 PM
To: Don Sublett
Subject: RE: 17 Aug. Update... I am Home

Don,

As I told Curt, I don't know if I could have handled things as well as you have. Sorry I have not been around to come visit. Please know you are in my prayers each day.

Lee

-----Original Message-----
From: Don Sublett
Sent: Thursday, August 17, 8:41 PM
To: Lee G.
Subject: RE: 17 Aug. Update... I am Home

Lee,

Your faith and prayer will make all the difference during the tough times.

Don

-----Original Message-----
From: Jane Keller
Sent: Friday, August 18, 8:33 AM
To: Don Sublett
Subject: Re: 17 Aug. Update... I am Home

Wow; I am amazed you are feeling up to giving us such a detailed report and can remember so much of what has been done, and said! You are a pretty amazing ol' boy! And, an amazing example of faith! Joe will be home late tonight and has been keeping up with you long distance. Kristi has been in touch with Leslie and has gotten the daughter report of your adventure. We are all praying for you, as we have been, and will continue to do. Billy T. has been very in touch with all of your communication and always asks about you when I see him. You are right... a big support group that is not even visible!

Love to all,

Jane

-----Original Message-----
From: Don Sublett
Sent: Friday, August 18, 12:17 PM
To: Jane Keller
Subject: Re: 17 Aug. Update... I am Home

Jane,

It took a while to put all that together, but amazingly, I have felt pretty good throughout this experience. There have been moments, but overwhelmingly more good than bad. I also have been able to maintain a good level of calmness as we have rolled from one event to the next. I have to attribute all of that to the many prayers God has answered on my behalf.

Michael and I went out to Eglin, earlier, and got the second neck drain removed. I now just have tape on the neck, with nothing protruding from it. I am hopeful I will have healed enough by Wednesday that she will be able to remove the sutures.

Think I am going to settle in, watch some golf this afternoon, and take it easy for the next couple of days.

Hope Joe makes it in safely. Come see us.

We love you all,

Don

VII.

More Answered Prayer

-----Original Message-----
From: Don Sublett
Sent: Wednesday, August 23, 3:47 PM
To: Support Group
Subject: 23 Aug. Update

Hi Everyone!

Just returned from getting the sutures removed and Dr. McMurphy had the pathology reports back already. There was no cancer in any of the 40 lymph nodes which were removed, nor was there any cancer in the tongue. Praise God for answered prayer!

I will follow with more later, but Judy and I are certainly tremendously relieved and very thankful.

Praise the Lord!

Don

-----Original Message-----
From: Brenda F.
Sent: Wednesday, August 23, 4:47 PM
To: Don Sublett
Subject: Re: 23 Aug. Update

Oh, Don!

How wonderful! God would have still been wonderful, even if there had been cancer, but I am sure thankful that He's not asking you to walk that road! Thanks for letting me know. I will pass the news on to my links.

God bless!

Sis

-----Original Message-----
From: Don Sublett
Sent: Wednesday, August 23, 5:00 PM
To: Brenda F.
Subject: Re: 23 Aug. Update

Sis,

It was good news and we are so thankful to get it. Answered prayer!

Don

-----Original Message-----
From: Dawn S.
Sent: Wednesday, August 23, 3:46 PM
To: Don Sublett
Subject: Re: 23 Aug. Update

Oh, we are *so* happy for you! Is it completely conclusive? Cancer gone? Or just what they could see?

Dawn

-----Original Message-----
From: Don Sublett
Sent: Wednesday, August 23, 5:00 PM
To: Dawn S.
Subject: Re: 23 Aug. Update

Dawn,

We are tremendously thankful, as well. None of the scans will detect anything smaller than 5mm in size. From that standpoint, it is possible there is cancer somewhere in the body. That is why I will be followed especially close the first two years. However, there was none discovered in the lymph nodes or in the primary site. So, I am as clean as can be determined.

Don

-----Original Message-----
From: Laurie Willcox
Sent: Wednesday, August 23, 4:30 PM
To: Don Sublett
Subject: Re: 23 Aug. Update

Yeah! What wonderful news! I know the sense of relief and accomplishment you must feel with this news. I am so happy for you!

Love,

Laurie

-----Original Message-----
From: Don Sublett
Sent: Wednesday, August 23, 9:19 PM
To: Laurie Willcox
Subject: Re: 23 Aug. Update

Laurie,

We are tremendously relieved and appreciative of all the answered prayer. I think you know
exactly how we feel, and it feels pretty good.

Love you all,

Don

-----Original Message-----
From: Jim B.
Sent: Wednesday, August 23, 3:20 PM
To: Don Sublett
Subject: RE: 23 Aug. Update

Don,

That is outstanding news. I am sure your Dr.
will recommend aggressive monitoring. I am also
sure you will stay on top of it, too.

Jim

-----Original Message-----
From: Don Sublett
Sent: Wednesday, August 23, 9:21 PM
To: Jim B.
Subject: RE: 23 Aug. Update

Jim,

We are, obviously, tremendously relieved to get the news. I have terrific docs, as you know, and Dr. McMurphy will see me once a month for the first year, every two months the second year, etc. She will also repeat the CT/PET scan in six months. This cancer normally comes back within the first two years, if it returns. So, you can bet we will be staying on top of it as much as is humanly possible.

Don

-----Original Message-----
From: Gerda Rorabaugh
Sent: Wednesday, August 23, 5:17 PM
To: Don Sublett
Subject: RE: 23 Aug. Update

"Praise the Lord!" is right. The best news we got in a long time. What a relief it must be for all of you, as it is for us. We had faith all the way, but at times wondered just how much the doctors could do. With God's help, they did an excellent job and now you are on the way to recovery. Please keep us updated on how your recovery progress goes.

Still in our thoughts and prayers.

Love,

Gerda and Bill

-----Original Message-----
From: Don Sublett
Sent: Wednesday, August 23, 9:23 PM
To: Gerda Rorabaugh
Subject: RE: 23 Aug. Update

Gerda and Bill,

We are greatly relieved and very appreciative of the answered prayer. There is still some healing to be done, but I think being out from under the stress will accelerate the process.

Love you all,

Don

-----Original Message-----
From: J.C.
Sent: Thursday, August 24, 2006 6:00 AM
To: Don Sublett
Subject: RE: 23 Aug. Update

Don,

I am sitting in my hotel room, in Korea (at Ulchi Focus Lens), and this is absolutely great news. Thanks be to God! I am so happy for you and know that through this journey you will emerge even stronger.

J.C.

-----Original Message-----
From: Don Sublett
Sent: Thursday, August 24, 8:00 AM
To: J.C.
Subject: RE: 23 Aug. Update

J.C.,

That is about the most distant e-mail I have received. Ha! Enjoy the time in Korea.

It was wonderful news and we are greatly relieved to receive it. God has blessed us tremendously these last several months. Now, I have to get back on a normal diet and get the feeding tube and chemo port removed. The throat has begun to ease a bit, already, so I think the next couple weeks should see some great strides.

We appreciate the prayers!

Don

-----Original Message-----
From: Sanford Flach
Sent: Thursday, August 24, 6:14 AM
To: Don Sublett
Subject: Re: I received the update.

Hi Don,

We are so happy to hear that everyone's prayers have been answered. I was, however, surprised to hear they removed 40 nodes. No wonder your surgery was much longer than mine. They only removed two of mine. We pray you will continue along the road to recovery.

Sanford

-----Original Message-----
From: Don Sublett
Sent: Thursday, August 24, 9:10 AM
To: Sanford Flach
Subject: Re: I received the update.

Sanford,

You know how it feels—every bit of this, from the onset to the conclusion. We certainly feel a great sense of relief and gratitude.

I don't think she was willing to take any chances of the cancer spreading, if it was there, and that is why she took out so many nodes. She is aggressive every step of the way.

My gag reflex has relaxed quite a bit, this past week. I am sitting here getting ready to try and eat a piece of toast. I will try to force something down at every mealtime, from here on. I want to have this tube out in two weeks.

I sure do appreciate the support you provided along the way. Sharing your experience was very helpful to me in a lot of ways. I also want to thank you for the prayers. We know God answered a lot of them in my behalf. Let's stay in touch.

Don

****

-----Original Message-----
From: Don Sublett
Sent: Wednesday, August 23, 10:21 PM
To: Al J.; Jim A.; Mike B; Glenn G.; T. Carter; Ray Willcox
Cc: Chip L.; Stan N.; Paula Willcox
Subject: Sunday Morning

Brothers,

I would like to address the congregation, *briefly*, during the response time, Sunday morning. Then, if it is ok, I would like Chip to lead #96, "I Stand In Awe," immediately following my comments. I don't know that the song needs to go in the bulletin, but just that I would like it to be sung following my comments.

Don

It was a tremendous joy to be able to stand before the church family and express Judy's and my personal thanks for the support: cards, letters, visits, e-mails, food, and most importantly, their prayers. That was a moment I looked forward to for months.

As I took the podium, I mentioned to the congregation that it was almost six months ago to the day since I had been diagnosed with Stage 4 cancer and the good news was that just a couple of days ago I had been declared cancer free. Immediately, a spontaneous round of applause broke out and my heart swelled with gratitude to God.

As I looked out on the faces of many who had been so supportive during that difficult time, there were two points I wanted to make. First, I wanted the church family to know just how much Judy and I appreciated the fact that we were *never* alone. We felt the prayers and knew we could have called on any of them at any time, for anything. Second, I wanted them to know the only reason I made it through treatment without the normal, painful and debilitating side-effects, like those Dr. Prieto described to me, and was healed of the cancer, was because of God answering their prayers, and the prayers of many others, on my behalf. There is no other explanation. (Of the nine head-and-neck cancer patients I now know of, I am the only one who escaped having the painful and debilitating side-effects.)

As an expression of thanks to God, I asked them to help me express my thanksgiving and awe to God, because of the way He had blessed me throughout. The best way I knew how was to sing, "I Stand in Awe," and we did. There were tears in my eyes.

****

-----Original Message-----
From: Don Sublett
Sent: Wednesday, August 23, 10:21 PM
To: Support Group
Subject: Final Update - 26 Aug.

Good Evening Friends,

It has been a couple days since I started this. I was out of commission, yesterday, because lightning hit the house Thursday night and took out my computer, satellite dish, and coffee pot. I suppose we are fortunate more damage was not done.

I have had over twenty-four hours for the news I am cancer free to sink in. I think I am still getting used to that fact. These last six months have been pretty intense at times, and I am still feeling some of the effects of the "cure." Still, it is wonderful to know the cancer has been killed and our lives, while they will never be quite the same again, are returning to a less frantic and uncertain state.

I honestly believe I might have been in a bit of shock, Wednesday, when Dr. McMurphy gave me the news. I was not expecting to hear anything for at least another week or two. For some reason, the pathologist at Eglin elected to study the tissue instead of send it to the Air Force Institute of Pathology (AFIP). From what Dr. Mac said, there appears to be no intention to send it to AFIP for further study. This is apparently good news, because it means there is no doubt about the absence of cancer. If there was any concern they would definitely be sending it off for a second opinion.

Dr. Mac told me she received the report on Tuesday, but said she didn't want to give me the pathology news, good or bad, over the phone. She knew I was coming in to have the sutures removed, on Wednesday, and elected to wait for my scheduled appointment. Dr. Mac was clearly elated to be able to relate good news, because it doesn't always work out that way.

Dr. Mac is insistent that I not return to work until October 2nd. There is some healing which needs to occur to my neck, as well as from the handling of the nerves during surgery. I also still have a considerable amount of swelling from the radiation. She wants me to get my strength back, gain some weight and get off the feeding tube. To enable the latter, I have committed to eating something by mouth at each meal time. The gag reflex has improved significantly this past week, but in order to get back to normal, I have to pretty much teach myself to overcome the choking reflex, which occurs when food hits the back of the throat, sort of like the old, "use it or lose it" saying. It has been a while since my throat was really exercised and I lost control over the gag reflex. So, I have to regain that control. These are small problems in the overall scheme of things.

As I wrap things up in these next few paragraphs, I come back to one thing which has been said before. Many have continued to tell me they are not certain they could deal with cancer as I have. As mentioned previously, you will either fight cancer—or something else equally significant—or give in to it. I don't see any middle ground. When the confrontation occurs, I think almost everyone will choose to fight it to the extent of their ability and their faith. Also, if we accept the reality that we will one day die, we have an opportunity to prepare ourselves, both spiritually and physically, for the battles and struggles which will occur. As we grow older, our faith ought to be increasing as we depend less on ourselves and more on our God.

There have also been those I have encountered who set a tremendous example for me, young and old alike. My parents both died comfortable in their faith in God. There was also a good friend of ours, from Alaska, Jack Esslinger. Jack was diagnosed with a brain tumor which eventually killed him. In discussing his cancer and what to pray for, Jack asked me that I pray he would be able to handle whatever side effects came with grace and dignity. I prayed that prayer often for Jack and God gave him the strength to deal with the adversities which occurred as his condition diminished physically. I have also prayed, often, that same prayer for myself, over the years. I also reflect on a young lady we went to church with in Niceville. Her name was Chardon White. Chardon was less than twenty when diagnosed with cancer. She was such an example of faith that I still tear up on occasion when I think about how she demonstrated her Christian faith. Chardon went into remission and then came out after only a brief time. Yet, her faith never wavered. I think everyone who knew Chardon learned a tremendous amount from her about how to deal with death. Then, there is Laurie Willcox. Laurie is the daughter-in-law of very good friends of ours, Ray and Paula. She was not yet thirty and a fairly new mom when diagnosed with an aggressive form of breast cancer. Laurie chose to fight the cancer and made some, I think, particularly difficult choices during the course of her treatment. She beat her cancer and is a shining example of faith in Christ. (She is also the one whom I got the idea of updates by e-mail from.) There are many others who have made an impact on me that I could also mention, but, without being maudlin, the point is we have an opportunity to prepare ourselves for the inevitable, if we choose to do so. I encourage you to do that.

Once again, please pay attention to what is going on in your body and don't be afraid to confront it. Early detection is key to living to fight another day. I most certainly testify to that. Though my cancer was in Stage 4 when it was discovered, it was early in Stage 4. Had I waited to pursue getting that swollen and sore lymph node checked, I might not have been so fortunate.

I hope, after seeing how God blessed me these last six months, that no one doubts God answers prayer. I believe God has been involved from the onset of the swollen/cancerous lymph node right on through to today. I also firmly believe your prayers were key in God preventing me from having the normal painful and debilitating effects from the radiation to the head and neck, and then God laying His healing hands upon me. Yes, I had excellent doctors and some of the best medical treatment available, but it is ultimately in God's hands. So, I feel extraordinarily blessed because of the events of these past six months.

At times, words are so inadequate to fully express the gratitude that you feel. Yet, when trying to do so by e-mail, they are all we have. So, please know there are tears in my eyes as I sit here typing these last few sentences. These are tears of gratitude and thanksgiving for the love, concern, help, and prayers offered for Judy and me these last six months. You—and your friends—made the daily path so much easier to walk, and then God carried us in His arms during the especially difficult times. We were *never* alone.

Judy and I wish God's richest blessings upon you.

With deep and abiding Christian love to each of you—our friends,

Don

-----Original Message-----
From: Bruce Nunnally
Sent: Saturday, August 26, 4:23 PM
To: Don Sublett
Subject: RE: Final Update - 26 Aug.

Don,

Great final update! It is an inspiration. I am a big believer in, it is not *what* happens in our lives which God is so concerned about, but *how we react* to what happens in our lives that God is so concerned about. You have shown that you dealt with this adversity in a serious, fighting, don't-give-up way, but at the same time, you dealt with it in an accepting, prepared, realistic way. To me, that shows great wisdom. You have also shown your never-bending faith in the Father. Thanks for your inspiration.

Bruce

-----Original Message-----
From: Don Sublett
Sent: Saturday, August 26, 4:49 PM
To: Bruce Nunnally
Subject: RE: Final Update - 26 Aug.

Bruce,

Thank you for such kind words. I dealt with the situation in the only way I knew how. We serve a wonderful God who truly loves us and wants to be involved in our lives, if we will just let Him.

Don

-----Original Message-----
From: John Fuhrmann
Sent: Saturday, August 26, 6:37 PM
To: Don Sublett
Subject: Re: Final Update - 26 Aug.

Don & Judy,

Congratulations to both of you for showing all of us what dignity, grit, faith, and trust in our Creator really mean when the stakes are as high as they get. You are both stronger for what you have endured and conquered. Hopefully, many years of health and happiness now lie ahead!

Cheers and happiness to you,

John & Bette

-----Original Message-----
From: Don Sublett
Sent: Saturday, August 26, 9:01 PM
To: John Fuhrmann
Subject: Re: Final Update - 26 Aug.

John and Bette,

If your faith is not there in the end, then it is going to be pretty grim. We are stronger for what we have endured and sure hope we don't have any more trials like this for a while. The road ahead looks bright and we are thankful for that.

We do appreciate your support, encouragement, and prayers these last several months. You
made the road easier for us to travel, and I mean
that.

Don

-----Original Message-----
From: Jane Keller
Sent: Saturday, August 26, 9:29 PM
To: Don Sublett
Subject: Re: Final Update - 26 Aug.

Now, that made me cry! Maybe you should
go into writing inspirational literature as a
profession!

Still loving you all,

Jane

-----Original Message-----
From: Don Sublett
Sent: Saturday, August 26, 9:51 PM
To: Jane Keller
Subject: Re: Final Update - 26 Aug.

Jane,

I don't know that I have a lot of those in me.
If the case, I had better save them for when they
are needed.
We love you all and appreciate having
prayer warriors like you on our side. I know God
does, too!

Don

-----Original Message-----
From: Marilyn Jones
Sent: Sunday, August 27, 8:19 PM
To: Don Sublett
Subject: Re: Final Update - 26 Aug.

Dear Don,

I was crying before I finished reading your letter. I bet you made a lot of people cry. Writing that letter was a nice thing to do. I am so thankful for the cancer-free diagnosis. Even though we haven't kept in touch until recently, Leslie has been a special part of my life, both as a child and as an adult. She was so sweet when she was in my class and she still is.

If you get to Alaska again, let us know. We are gone a lot, but I check e-mail wherever I am. We would be happy to provide you and Judy a place to stay if our house is not already full. One cousin has made reservations for two years from now!

Love,

Marilyn

-----Original Message-----
From: Don Sublett
Sent: Monday, August 28, 8:31 AM
To: Marilyn Jones
Subject: Re: Final Update - 26 Aug.

Marilyn,

It was probably just the soft-hearted folks who might have cried a little bit. I got an incredible amount of support via e-mail during the past six months. If people only knew what the little notes and words of encouragement meant to someone going through a difficult time, there would be an awful lot more of them. We have been incredibly blessed, time and again, during this experience with my cancer. One of the ways was just re-establishing contact with a lot of people from our past. That has been one of the most enjoyable aspects.

You mentioned Leslie. She is something else. She is like my mother in one respect. I don't think she has ever met a stranger. She just takes to people and people take to her. We have been very fortunate that both she and Michael have good marriages and they are all active in the church. They seem to know what is important and we are very thankful for that.

I would love to make at least one more trip to Alaska, but don't know when, or if, that might occur. We used to make Bill and Jan's home our base when they were up there. They always seemed like they enjoyed having us. Bill and Jan are over in Pensacola now. We have seen them a couple times, though not recently. However, they have called several times to check on me. Jan and Bill haven't changed a bit over the years. We will certainly keep your offer in mind. It is very kind of you.

Again, we have appreciated the thought and prayers so very much these past several months. It was wonderful knowing so many people were engaged in this battle with us. I will certainly keep you informed if anything warrants, but will also plan to stay in touch.

Our love to you and Jerry,

Don and Judy

-----Original Message-----
From: Andrea Plunk
Sent: Monday, August 28, 9:44 AM
To: Don Sublett
Subject: RE: Final Update - 26 Aug.

Don,

You were never alone and we will always be inspired to grow from what you have written. I love a happy ending!

Thanks,

Andrea

-----Original Message-----
From: Don Sublett
Sent: Monday, August 28, 9:43 AM
To: Andrea Plunk
Subject: RE: Final Update - 26 Aug.

Andrea,

I do hope that in some small way I will have been able to help some others to face adversity. It is made much easier when you have friends and family working out things with God on your behalf. He sure has blessed us these last several months!

Love you all,

Don

-----Original Message-----
From: Pat and Bob Coonfield
Sent: Tuesday, August 29, 10:20 AM
To: Don Sublett
Subject: God is great!

Dear Don and Judy:

Our joy in reading your e-mail, yesterday, still brings tears to our eyes. We seldom have the internet available to us as we travel, but we are staying at the church in Evansville, IN, while visiting my mother. I confiscated their phone and got caught-up (on e-mail). I am telling you this so you will understand the emotional roller coaster we were on yesterday. We had 47 pieces of mail and I read them as they were written, not jumping ahead to find out the results. So Patty and I cried as we read each one of your epistles. Then cried for real joy and thanksgiving as we read the last one.

I have learned when a loved one is ill to pray for their recovery, but equally important to pray that some good may come from their illness. I am convinced both prayers have been answered in you. The bravery and faith in our God, which you demonstrated, has taught your brothers, sisters, and co-workers a priceless lesson. One that I pray I am able to imitate should the opportunity present itself.

We love you both so very much and share your happiness. Our prayers continue with you as you go into therapy. Lord willing, we will see you in October.

Love,

Bob and Pat

-----Original Message-----
From: Don Sublett
Sent: Tuesday, August 29, 2:03 PM
To: Pat and Bob Coonfield
Subject: God is great!

Bob and Pat,

Great to hear from you! Hope all is going well with your visit in Indiana. I appreciate the very kind and thoughtful words. Judy and I were obviously very thrilled to get the news last week. God has incredibly blessed us throughout this entire experience, from start to finish, whenever the finish might be. It has been unique to be able to share the experience with so many people. I think there are quite a few who really appreciated and benefited from being able to follow along through the cancer experience with us. But, I think we benefited far more than anyone else did. The blessings we received from being able to share were almost beyond belief. The age of the internet is remarkable.

There have been quite a few prayers offered for you all, and your (potential) converts, in Bowling Green, so by doing that, we have also been remembering you in your travels. I know you will be glad to get back home for a while and we will be glad to welcome you back.

Safe travels and God's blessings,

Don

-----Original Message-----
From: Stephen G.
Sent: Monday, August 28, 3:56 PM
To: Don Sublett
Subject: Amen

Don,

Welcome back from the brink. I followed your progress through Rocky's updates. I have a hard time expressing myself to someone in your situation and chose to monitor from afar, but please note that I did think and pray for you often. All I can say is you are one heck of a fighter, and I am so very happy to hear you beat the beast.

Best Wishes!

Steve

From: Don Sublett
Sent: Monday, August 28, 9:33 PM
To: Steve G.
Subj: RE: Amen

Steve,

I appreciate the note and also knowing you were thinking of and praying for me. I was tremendously blessed because of many people just like you. It's obvious God heard the prayers of so many and answered them.

I'm looking forward to being able to return to work. That's when things will really start to look and feel just a bit more normal again.

Don

****

-----Original Message-----
From: Don Sublett
Sent: Tuesday, October 03, 8:29 PM
To: Support Group
Subject: Just a Note

Good Evening Everyone!

I have received several inquiries the last few days, asking how I am doing, so I thought I would provide a brief note to update you. In a word, I am doing superb. The neck incision has healed very nicely from the surgery, though there is still quite a bit of swelling, numbness, and tightness along the incision. Dr. McMurphy has me applying an ointment three times a day to the incision, to help loosen and stretch the skin. There is occasional mild pain and stiffness in the right shoulder from the surgery, but it is certainly tolerable. The nerves have some healing to do and it could still be months before the nerves come back to normal, but Dr. Mac once again assured me during my monthly visit that all the nerves are intact. So, it seems to be just a matter of time. She also told me I will get a CT/PET scan every six months for the next couple of years. Since there are no markers for this type cancer, the CT/PET will be a major tool in early detection, should cancer crop up anywhere in the body.

The chemo port was removed a little over a week ago and it was good to get it out. However, I still have the feeding tube. Dr. Mac says once I am taking everything by mouth and gaining weight she will consent to having the tube removed. I am hopeful it will be out by the end of the month and see no reason why it will not be.

I have made tremendous strides the last couple of weeks in taking food by mouth. The throat, though not fully open yet, is opening up some, and the gag reflex is easing. I am eating just about everything on the menu, though it is slow going, because I have to thoroughly chew everything in order to swallow it. That is not all bad. The only thing the feeding tube has been used for the last couple of weeks is as a means to take my Prilosec each evening. It is in capsule form and I haven't gotten my courage up yet to try and swallow the capsule, so I crush the pellets and use the tube. Guess I need to try and swallow the capsule, huh? I will in the next couple of days. I promise.

I went back to work, yesterday. That was a major milestone on the road to the "new normal." Dr. Mac did well by me when she insisted I have six weeks after surgery to recover. I needed the time and these last couple weeks have shown major improvement in my physical stamina. This improvement also probably coincides with the return to a somewhat normal diet. It felt good to be back in the swing of things.

As I wrap things up, let me make a plea to you to have regular check-ups—men and women, both. As an example, a work buddy had a full colonoscopy today and they found several small polyps, as well as a couple about 5mm, which were all removed. He will repeat the scope in six to eight months, as a precaution. The reason we have check-ups is to find things before they become serious problems.

Also, please keep in mind there is a reason cancer is called the *"silent killer."* It is my understanding that, generally, cancer doesn't hurt until it has metastasized and gotten into organs and/or nerves and starts to cause problems, and pain. I was very fortunate. Recall, the only time I felt any pain from my cancer was the morning last

December, when I woke up with that swollen and sore lymph node? Had I not paid attention and followed up, I might not have been so fortunate as to have been able to kill the cancer before it killed me.

So, things are coming back to what I term the "new normal." I don't see how life can ever be the same after going through treatment for cancer. There is a much keener appreciation for life each day, just as there is for what Christ did by going to the cross for each of us. Judy and I appreciate so very much the support, love, and encouragement you provided these last seven months. Make no mistake, God heard your prayers and answered them, and we are very thankful to you, and to Him!

God's richest blessings to you,

Don

-----Original Message-----
From: Jane Keller
Sent: Tuesday, October 03, 8:45 PM
To: Don Sublett
Subject: Re: Just a Note

Thanks so much for filling in the blanks and answering the unasked questions. We continue to pray for you every day, as do so many others, I am sure. It is encouraging to "see" you in such good spirits after a trying ordeal. I know it feels good to be back at work.

Love to all,

Jane

-----Original Message-----
From: Don Sublett
Sent: Tuesday, October 03, 8:56 PM
To: Jane Keller
Subject: Re: Just a Note

Jane,

Those prayers are still very much needed and appreciated. Keep them going up! I have an awful lot to be thankful for. I hesitate to say I am cured, because the scans only show tumors 5mm or larger, so I tell folks we killed the cancer we know about, but I don't live under a cloud of worry. I live under a sky of thankfulness.

Hope we can get over and see you all before long. We need to have a celebratory dinner at the Bonefish Grill. We will not make it this weekend, because we plan to go to Baton Rouge. We might try to make it the next one, if you all will be home.

Don

-----Original Message-----
From: Mike Bagwell
Sent: Tuesday, October 03, 9:38 PM
To: Don Sublett
Subject: RE: Just a Note

And the great news just keeps coming! All praise to God! His hand was surely involved from the start. As you say, you've gotten a second chance.

Glad to hear you were able to go back to work. That is a significant milestone. Remember the roses along the path; stop to smell them occasionally.

Mike

-----Original Message-----
From: Don Sublett
Sent: Tuesday, October 03, 9:42 PM
To: Mike Bagwell
Subject: RE: Just a Note

Mike,

Things continue to go extremely well. The throat is really starting to relax. Getting my ability to eat back has been a challenge, but things are smoothing out on that front, too. I will take a deep breath when the feeding tube is out. That will speak volumes about the progress made.

You can bet I am smelling the roses. Hope I never forget to stop and do that.

Don

-----Original Message-----
From: Travis Huffman
Sent: Tuesday, October 03, 10:22 PM
To: Don Sublett
Subject: Re: Just a Note

Don,

Let me begin with an apology. Over the past few months, Linda and I have been following your case very closely and praying for your recovery on a regular basis. The apology is for not letting you know about our prayers. Doug has also been involved in much of your recovery through prayers. I have forwarded several of your e-mails to him.

Linda and I cannot tell you how thankful we are that you have recovered so well. But, most of all, we have been blessed as we took an interest in your health. I work with a hospice company and counsel many of the patients concerning their illness and their upcoming death. Your attitude and approach to your illness has been truly an educational and encouraging experience for us. Your positive attitude and spiritual confidence has shown through all your suffering. I have never seen anyone have a better understanding of the power of prayer. Thank you for allowing us to take part in your deepest thoughts as you went through perhaps the most difficult time in your life on this earth.

In Christian love,

Travis

-----Original Message-----
From: Don Sublett
Sent: Wednesday, October 04, 9:25 PM
To: Travis Huffman
Subject: Re: Just a Note

Travis,

No apology needed. It is just good to hear from you and learn things are going well with you all. You are in a very tough line of work, but one you are no doubt good at. It has to be tough to see people dying and not be part of the Lord's family. I know you must experience that from time-to-time.

I am glad reading my e-mails has been of benefit to you. I can assure you that writing them was beneficial to me. It helped me to sort through feelings and to confront the reality of my situation. I have also learned the true goodness of God—the fact that He sent Christ to die on the cross. Due to that fact, we will never die. That is the real blessing.

Judy and I are living in Niceville, FL, which is near Destin and Fort Walton Beach, in the

Panhandle. Our daughter, Leslie, and her family, live in Alexandria, VA. Michael and his family now live in Rochester, NY. Les has one daughter and Michael has two. All are involved in the church and are doing well.

It would seem we are blessed on all fronts and are very fortunate.

Again, good to hear from you all. Please stay in touch.

Don

****

Once again, I felt compelled to pass along to the (new) Eglin AFB Hospital Commander just what wonderful medical care I had received from her people. I cannot say enough good about the dedicated healthcare professionals who took care of me!

From: Don Sublett
Sent: Wednesday, October 04, 3:09 PM
To: Van Decar Tama R Col MIL USAF 96 MDG/CC
Subject: An Appreciative Note... though a bit long.

Colonel Van Decar,

Ma'am, I am compelled to write you about my recent *successful* treatment at the Eglin AFB hospital for squamous cell base-of-tongue cancer. These past seven months saw me in the care of some of the finest doctors, nurses, technicians, and professionals in the United States Air Force, as well as in our local civilian community. I can just barely begin to adequately compliment and commend the wonderful people you lead, as well as those professionals in the civilian community you partner with to provide health care. They are second to none!

My primary Eglin physicians were Dr. (Maj.) Andrea McMurphy, Otolaryngology, Dr. (Maj.) Brian Moore, and Dr. (Lt. Col.) Robert Prieto, Oncology. Dr. Prieto separated and was replaced by Dr. (Maj.) Alison Gorrebeeck. Additionally, I was sent to 21st Century Radiation Oncology, in Fort Walton Beach, for radiation therapy under the care of Dr. Joseph Bonanno.

There were many people, both at Eglin and in Fort Walton Beach, integral in my treatment who stood out. The doctors and staff at 21st Century Radiation Oncology: Dr. Bonanno, Teri and Nancy (nurses), and the technicians, Mark, Linda, Sheri, and Brandi, set the standard with their abilities and the level of care provided. I find it remarkable that the techs put me on the table in the same exact position for each treatment, but they did. Additionally, they always told me what was being done and when to likely expect changes in side-effects from the radiation. No surprises are wanted or needed when undergoing treatment for cancer, and they made sure I didn't experience any.

I was all over the Eglin hospital these past months: ENT, Oncology, Surgery Clinic, Internal Medicine, ASU/MSU, Nutrition, Surgical Ward, Radiology, Pathology, Lab/Serology, and the Pharmacy. You should know that every single person I came in contact with in your hospital provided the most personalized care and support imaginable. I can honestly say I lacked for nothing and I did not have a single unpleasant or disappointing experience, nor did I witness any unpleasantries dispensed by your people to anyone else. I find that remarkable.

Among your standouts are SSgt. Venus Osborne and Ms. Phyllis Bernier, in Oncology. SSgt. Osborne is one of the most pleasant and efficient technicians in the Eglin Hospital. There was nothing she wouldn't do to assist in my treatment. Additionally, Ms. Bernier has to be one of the best Oncology nurses in the nation. In addition to efficiently administering the chemotherapy, she is current on the therapies and is an encyclopedia of knowledge on outcomes, side-effects, and how to reduce or eliminate them. What a treasure!

I must also include Dr. Gorrebeeck among the standouts. I was impressed in my initial visits with Dr. Prieto and was equally impressed with Dr. Gorrebeeck, when she assumed responsibility for my treatment and care in Oncology. She stepped right in when Dr. Prieto left and we never missed a beat. Dr. Gorrebeeck continues to monitor my condition and routinely follows up. I appreciate that.

One of your nutritionists, 1Lt. Eva-Maria Schwebel, spent considerable time with me, working up a nutrition plan which would enable me to maximize the benefit of the feeding tube. Every doctor commented, throughout, how well I was handling the treatments and how healthy I looked. My superb physical condition was due in large part to Lt. Schwebel's efforts in helping me develop a good nutrition plan.

I had three surgeries during my cancer treatment: the initial tongue biopsy, in March; insertion of the Medi-port and feeding tube, in April; and another tongue biopsy and lymph node dissection in August. Two of the surgeries required being admitted. The nurses and technicians in the ASU/MSU and on the surgical ward treated me just like they would want to be treated if in my position. When you "Do unto others..." you can't go wrong. I assure you, they did not do any wrong at all.

Finally, Dr. McMurphy. I suppose it is only natural to have a keen affinity for someone so integrally involved in saving your life, but Dr. McMurphy is the best! She instills confidence with her aggressive approach and backs it up with performance. I relaxed after that first visit, when Dr. McMurphy told me, "I have scheduled the OR tomorrow for a tongue biopsy. We can cancel if I am going too fast." I assured her faster was better and put myself in her hands. She never let me down.

Dr. McMurphy pushed for aggressive radiation therapy treatment of the neck, following protocols established at academic cancer centers, and convinced Dr. Bonanno the team could support a patient through such an aggressive regimen in the community setting. When "hot spots" showed on the post-treatment CT/PET scan, Dr. McMurphy performed surgery soon thereafter to determine if any cancer remained. She was very candid, prior to the surgery, in discussing possible future surgery to the tongue if cancer remained and advised that, if required, it would be a surgery Dr. Moore would perform. That discussion reinforced my confidence in her. It also bolstered my confidence in Dr. McMurphy and Dr. Moore as a surgical team. Dr. McMurphy and Dr. Moore are professional and dedicated to patient care to the point where they purchase medical/surgical instruments "out of pocket" in order to make certain they can do the best possible for their patients. You are fortunate to have Dr. McMurphy and Dr. Moore on your staff.

Fortunately, I am now cancer free! I know it is due in large part to the efforts of the entire Eglin AFB Hospital staff, but especially to the teams in ENT, Eglin Oncology, and 21st Century Radiation Oncology. I also know I will be followed closely for the next five years and am confident that, as long as I remain in the care of people like Dr. McMurphy, I will receive the best treatment possible.

I know that, ultimately, God is in control. However, I also realize He has blessed me at this particular time in my life by placing me in the midst of a wonderful and professional military healthcare community which is totally focused on patient care. For that, I am extremely thankful.

Very respectfully,

Donald W. Sublett, Major (R.), USAF

-----Original Message-----
From: Van Decar Tama R. Col. MIL USAF 96 MDG/CC
Sent: Thursday, October 05, 8:26 AM
To: Don Sublett
Subject: RE: An Appreciative Note... though a bit long.

Sir,

You have made my day! The people on staff at the Medical Group are the finest in the world. Your timing is impeccable, because the Deputy Surgeon General for the Armed Forces Medical Service is visiting us this week. I was trying to tell him last night that we need more surgical specialists, not less. Perhaps, I will just show him your e-mail... it is printing now. Beyond that, the people make the hospital, and the surgeons, nurses, physicians, and techs you describe, are simply what make this hospital work so well. I will take the time to thank them. But, I thank you for taking the time to let me know.

Tama

From: Don Sublett
Sent: Thursday, October 05, 8:56 AM
To: Van Decar Tama R. Col. MIL USAF 96 MDG/CC
Subject: RE: An Appreciative Note... though a bit long.

Colonel Van Decar,

Thank you for such a warm response to my note! We are blessed to have access to what has to be some of the best medical care available anywhere. I will be forever grateful for the care provided by your people, particularly Dr. McMurphy. She stepped up to the plate to make sure I received the maximum dose of radiation in the neck. This was probably very significant in having a successful outcome, because I had an eleven-day break in the middle of treatment, due to weight-loss in the face and neck.

I will be glad to share my story with anyone you'd like. I think it very important that people know the caliber of care you provide.

Very respectfully,

Don Sublett

For those interested in how I knew the technicians put me on the table in the same position before starting radiation, I had my own "check" on them. After I was positioned, they left the room prior to starting the linear accelerator and beginning the treatment. When the accelerator rotated to the right, five o'clock position, for that first dose of radiation to begin, a laser beam from the ceiling hit the left side of the bite block stick that was protruding from my mouth. The beam was on the very edge of the stick. If I moved my lip or mouth the slightest bit to the right, the beam slid off the stick. (My head was immobilized by the mask, which was fastened to the table, so I could not move it the slightest amount.) Thus, by having the beam on the very edge of the stick when treatment started, I knew in my own mind that I was positioned correctly. Still, I find it exceptional that, even though I had my own check, they were able to put me on their marks each time and not deviate even one millimeter in the positioning.

****

From: Don Sublett
Sent: Thursday, October 19, 10:09 PM
To: Support Group
Subject: Finally!!!

Good Evening, Friends:

Had a couple of good doctor visits today, with my primary doctor (McMurphy) and in the General Surgery Clinic. Doctor McMurphy was very pleased with the progress since my last monthly visit. The neck incision continues to heal nicely and the nerve which controls the lower lip is responding well. She said previously it could take three months for the droopy lip to return to normal and it looks like that is going to be about right. Also, my eating ability continues to improve. I am just not able to gain any weight. I know a lot of you would pay a pretty penny to have such a problem, but she is not pleased with that. Since gaining weight was one of the criteria for being able to have the feeding tube removed, she was not overjoyed that I had an appointment in the Surgery Clinic this afternoon to discuss getting it taken out. However, we discussed the removal.

I told her it had been over three weeks since I had put any Ensure through the tube and I am doing everything by mouth, including medicines, and that I would not go back to the tube unless dire circum- stances cropped up. It looks like dire circumstances will not be occurring, at least in the near term. She is very reasonable and certainly understood why I would want to have it removed. So, Dr. Mac said she would support whatever decision the surgeon made. Then, when I went to see the surgeon, he told me it was her decision. I asked him to give her a call and discuss it. Bottom line is, her concern was the tube would be difficult to reinsert if, for some reason, I became unable to eat. The surgeon said both procedure and thinking had changed. The thinking now is it is probably easier to insert a tube the second time than it is to put it in the first time. The reasoning is the stomach is already attached to the abdominal wall. So, the bottom line is the feeding tube was removed today.

While not as painful as I had feared, removal was enough to get my attention. "Traction removal" means just that. You have to get a little traction on the tube and yank that puppy out! That is what he did. So, I sit here this evening with no foreign objects any longer implanted in my body. Though a bit sore, it is a good feeling to close that chapter of this saga. Slightly more than seven months ago, the tube was inserted, and I remain absolutely certain having the feeding tube put in was one of the smartest things I did.

An interesting side note regarding Dr. McMurphy, which endears her to me even more, if that is possible, is that she went against conventional thinking, locally, to ensure I got an additional boost of radiation. The concern of my radiation oncologist was the effects of the increase in radiation would likely be very debilitating and that Dr. Mac, and the folks on Eglin, might not be able to adequately support me. She stood firm and assured him they would take care of me, so they pressed ahead with the boost the last two weeks of radiation. We all know how well I handled the treatments, because of answered prayer, and how astounded everyone was. Now I know they were really astounded! What I had not considered, until this past week, was this significant boost in the amount of radiation likely overcame whatever recovery the cancer might have made during my eleven day break in treatments. Just further proof that, "All things work together for the good of those who love the Lord..."

This will be the last of my updates. I am back at work and in the final phases (I hope) of the healing processes. Each day now, life should be returning a little more to the "new normal." That will be a welcomed relief, especially considering the sometimes difficult periods of these past seven months. However, I assure you I will miss the frequent e-mail exchanges and other communications I have had with so many of you as we have fought this battle together. I cannot overstate the strength and encouragement you provided. As I pillow my head tonight, I will be thanking God for your love, support, and prayers. I ask that you thank Him for answering those prayers on my behalf.

With Christian love,

Don

-----Original Message-----
From: Wanda Nobles
Sent: Thursday, October 19, 10:22 PM
To: Don Sublett
Subject: Re: Finally!

Great news! I was just telling Mike, today, I needed to e-mail you and see how you are doing since you have been back to work. Is it good to be back, or is it exhausting? We were at Kinfolk's, today, and I reminded him I used to occasionally see you in there. We wondered if your sense of taste had returned enough for you to enjoy that kind of food yet. It sure was good!

Well, I will sure miss your e-mails, but I understand your need to get back to life, as usual! Take care of yourself and remember there are people here who would always love to hear from you whenever you have something to say!

I always thank God for you and for the work He has done in, and through, you.

Love you!

Wanda

-----Original Message-----
From: Don Sublett
Sent: Friday, October 20, 4:44 PM
To: Wanda Nobles
Subject: Re: Finally!

Wanda,

It is good to be back at work. I have a job which doesn't require me to have to "work." In that regard, I am very fortunate. So, it doesn't really tire me out.

As you point out, I forgot to mention the taste buds. They are still waffling a bit. Some days things taste pretty good. Other days they don't have much taste at all. We did our usual Friday thing at Kinfolk's, today, and I had the chicken sandwich and fries. This was the first time I tried a sandwich and it went down pretty easy. It also had a bit of taste. I didn't sauce it up, because my mouth is pretty sensitive to spices, at present. Seasonings are ok, but spices don't go over so well.

E-mail is a wonderful tool and it has really been beneficial to us; especially these last several months. Since the feeding tube has been removed,

I no longer have much to report on and am hopeful things will settle into a nice, uncomplicated routine. I do appreciate the interest so many have shown by wanting to keep up with developments and progress, but we have to wrap it up at some point so we don't become a "drag" on folks.

I always appreciate your responses because they are so heart-felt and genuine. You and Mike are wonderful people and we are blessed because of your friendship.

Love you all, too!

Don

-----Original Message-----
From: Carol D.
Sent: Friday, October 20, 9:48 AM
To: Don Sublett
Subject: Re: Finally!!!

I enjoyed receiving such good news. I know how pleased you are to no longer have the feeding tube inside you! Congratulations and my very best wishes.

Hopefully, this will not be your last e-mail update on the happenings in your life. However it is good to know the subject matter will be about a different road you are taking. You really are a good read and I have enjoyed learning more about you.

Love,

Carol

-----Original Message-----
From: Don Sublett
Sent: Friday, October 20, 5:00 PM
To: Carol D.
Subject: Re: Finally!!!

Carol,

You know we will continue to stay in touch, but I hope the future stories I might tell are not quite as dramatic as these last ones have been. We sure appreciate the support and help of the "Louisiana Bunch" these last several months.

We will see you next weekend,

Don

-----Original Message-----
From: Pat Rice
Sent: Friday, October 20, 3:06 PM
To: Don Sublett
Subject: Finally!!!

Don,

Only one thing to say, "Praise be to the Lord!" Now we have to remember—while our prayers for you were answered in a dramatic and measurable way—He answers our prayers every day, in perhaps a less striking way. I appreciate you sharing your journey with us and I rejoice with you, now, at the end of the road.

In Christian love,

Pat

-----Original Message-----
From: Don Sublett
Sent: Friday, October 20, 5:06 PM
To: Pat R.
Subject: Finally!!!

Pat,

Thanks for being part of the journey. I love my prayer warriors and know you are the leader of the pack! We continue to count our blessings, both great and small, and know God is good all of the time.

God Bless!

Don

-----Original Message-----
From: Topper Long
Sent: Monday, October 23, 5:26 PM
To: Don Sublett
Subject: Re: Finally!!!

Carole and I are so happy to get your *last* update—not because we don't enjoy hearing from you, but because of what it means to all of us—that you are *well!* We will continue to pray for you to be cancer-free for many years to come, and that you will have a happy, healthy, and enjoyable life. I am sure life truly has a new meaning for you that none of us who have not been down your path can really understand. Treasure and enjoy every day of it.

God bless you!

Topper

-----Original Message-----
From: Don Sublett
Sent: Monday, October 23, 5:26 PM
To: Topper Long
Subject: Re: Finally!!!

Topper,

I will most certainly appreciate the continued prayers. We hope you will not be strangers
down here, but will continue to stay in touch. We
certainly will.

Judy and I had dinner with Joe, Jane, and
Kristi, Saturday evening, and you all were a topic
of discussion, as always. I showed them the stone
Carole sent and told them what it meant to me.

As you suggest, there are certain shoes you
cannot walk in until you actually have to fit your
own pair. Still, I think we all appreciate life and
what it has to offer, especially as we reach certain
milestones in our lives. We are incredibly blessed
because of what the Lord did for us on the cross.
If we will always remember that fact alone, it will
make every day special.

Love and appreciate both you and Carol!

Don

-----Original Message-----
From: Mike Bagwell
Sent: Friday, October 20, 4:51 PM
To: Don Sublett
Subject: RE: Finally!!!

So good to hear of the success that prayer
brings! Don, I can tell you now, I thought you
were a *goner*. Everything sounded so bad when I

first heard from you. It is truly *amazing* how well you are doing now!

If you haven't realized it yet, God definitely has plans for you. You should consider updating us all in a year with what you have been doing, because, as I said, God's got plans for you.

Take care. Hope to see you soon—maybe Sunday.

Mike

-----Original Message-----
From: Don Sublett
Sent: Friday, October 20, 5:10 PM
To: Mike Bagwell
Subject: RE: Finally!!!

Mike,

I appreciate your candor. I don't know that I ever counted myself out, but knew the cancer was something I could not get through on my own. Fortunately, there were people like you and Penny who came on board and pestered the dickens out of God. I've said this to many people; I think God likes to be involved in our lives, if we will just let him.

I don't know what He has in store for me, but trust I will be able to tell my story far and wide. You have a good idea about providing an update in several months, or a year. I will plan on doing that.

Don

EPILOGUE

It has been almost four months since that last e-mail response and I have continued to see physical improvements, particularly in saliva production, my ability to eat and swallow, and in the taste buds. I felt all along that I would be able to resume eating a normal diet within two or three weeks after completing treatments, but this proved to be far too optimistic.

There was a major assault projected on my body through the chemo and radiation treatments. The throat was affected tremendously by the amount of radiation which it absorbed, especially the last two weeks of radiation treatment. Not putting any solid foods down the throat for an extended time affected the ability to swallow. I now seldom gag when swallowing and the possibility of choking is no longer a concern. Overcoming the hyper-active gag reflex took some time and effort, but major improvements in eating and swallowing have occurred this past month. As easy as swallowing has become, I expect further improvement in this area. Sanford has seen continued improvement in the after-effects of his treatment and it has been well over a year since his last treatment.

The taste buds have recovered significantly—to about sixty-percent of what they were before the radiation and chemo—but they are still playing games with me. Some days the taste buds are noticeably present and other days, everything tastes like flat Coca-Cola. Dr. Bonanno said the taste buds should recover to the extent they would within three months of my last radiation treatment. I was disappointed at the three month point, because I was not able to taste a lot of foods and when I was able to, the foods often had very little taste. However, taste has continued to improve beyond that three month point.

One annoying aspect of the taste bud recovery was my response to spicy foods. Eating anything spicy caused me to break out in an instant sweat. This response caused the taste buds to have to be re-trained. I can now eat medium spicy and well seasoned foods again. On the days when the taste buds are there, most other foods and beverages have at least a semblance of their normal taste and many sometimes have very good taste. Although, very few foods and beverages have the full bodied taste they did before chemo and radiation. I will be glad when the taste buds stabilize.

Saliva production has increased significantly and I am very thankful to Dr. Bonanno for the radiation treatment changes which enabled some recovery in the salivary glands. Whereas, most people I am aware of who underwent treatment similar to what I experienced have to carry a bottle of water around with them because of "dry mouth," I do not. I still don't have enough saliva to enable me to eat a meal without a beverage, but I have enough saliva production that swallowing is not too difficult. I can also hold an extended conversation without my mouth drying out.

Many people who undergo radiation to the head-and-neck also experience difficulty with being able to open their mouths very wide. This is due to the impact of the radiation on the muscles in the jaw. A normal person should be able to open his or her mouth wide enough to be able to insert three or four fingers vertically between the teeth. Whereas, Walt has a hard time inserting two fingers vertically into his mouth, I can easily insert three fingers. That one finger is the difference between being able to comfortably bite into a "Big Mac," or not. Swallowing, taste buds, and saliva, are the little things "normal people" tend to take for granted, because their abilities have never been compromised. For the head-and-neck cancer patient, they become significant areas of concern, because having them impaired affects our quality of life.

Some have asked me if there was any resentment because, as it turned out, the lymph node dissection proved to be unnecessary. My answer was, and remains an *emphatic*, "No!" I have extreme admiration and appreciation for all of my doctors and their aggressive approach to treating my cancer, especially Dr. McMurphy. Hindsight is supposed to be 20/20. So, it is easy to look back after the fact and say we should have waited, but when dealing with a Stage 4 cancer you do not have that luxury. In life, you have to make the best decision possible with the information at hand at the time.

Dr. McMurphy made the right decision when the CT/PET showed hot spots at the original tumor site and in the right side of the neck. There is an elementary fact which cannot be ignored when dealing with cancer. As long as cancer remains in the body, it will continue to grow, and possibly spread. The scan showed cancer could still be present and we went after it—no regrets, no remorse, just pure gratitude that the tissue showed clear of cancer!

I hope you gleaned from reading my experience with base-of-tongue cancer just how encouraged I was by those who responded to my updates. People kept telling me how encouraged they were by what I wrote. While I was glad to know that so many appreciated being kept abreast of my progress in treating the cancer, I unequivocally got far more encouragement from what I received in terms of kind thoughts, good wishes, and the knowledge so many were praying for my recovery, than they could have ever received from my writings.

E-mail and the internet are marvelous communication tools. I put out one message periodically and in-turn received dozens of replies to each one. I was genuinely strengthened by each response. It doesn't take much to build someone up. Just a short note which says you are thinking of and/or praying for someone is uplifting and encouraging.

The Eglin AFB Oncology Clinic is using me as a liaison to help their head-and-neck cancer patients deal with their cancer, and its treatment. I am grateful for the opportunity to help people who face a very difficult, and grave, situation. God blessed me in incredible ways during the entire course of my treatment. Just as Walt and Sanford helped me, I appreciate the opportunity to help others experiencing head-and-neck cancer, and to show them how God blessed me through the most difficult time of my life.

I don't know what the future holds, as far as a recurrence of the cancer, or another life-threatening disease. Whether we occasionally stop to think about it or not, we are always just one breath away from slipping into eternity. Dr. McMurphy told my wife and me that if the cancer recurs, it will most likely do so within the first two years after treatment. That is one reason why I will undergo a CT/PET scan every six months for at least the next two years.

I had my first follow-up CT/PET exam last week and met with Dr. McMurphy this morning to receive the results from the final report. I was told everything in the exam was "unremarkable" and was given a clean bill of health. While I had no indications the report results would be anything other than clean, there was a slight amount of apprehension as the "moment of truth," once again, approached. I suppose this is only normal and will continue as each follow-up exam is conducted.

As stated numerous times, ultimately, God is in control. I hope no one doubts that God answered prayer in my life during, and after, the time I was being treated for cancer. Of the nine other people I now know who have been treated for a head-and-neck cancer, I am the only one who experienced so little physical difficulty. Answered prayer is the only explanation for why the effects from my treatment were so benign. I remain absolutely certain that God wants to be deeply involved in our lives, if we will only let Him.

ADDENDUM

I am on the cusp of the tenth anniversary of the last radiation treatment, which I received on June 22, 2006. During the course of these last ten years, I have both known of and/or mentored about twenty-five men and women with Stage 4 head-and-neck cancer. To my knowledge, there are three of us who are still alive. In my own small sample and non-scientific way of doing the math, that equates to a little less than a 12 percent chance of long-term survival. Without doubt, head-and-neck cancer is a killer and that is why time is so crucial when you sense something may not be right!

When people ask me the reason I have fared so well when so many others have died, or do not have the quality of life I enjoy, I tell them I had good doctors, good medicine, and the Good Lord...not necessarily in that order.

I firmly believe that my survival and excellent quality-of-life is due to the power of prayer. When I speak of my experience to others it is always in the context of the Parable of the Persistent Widow in Luke 18:1-5. While we see how the Judge dealt with the widow's "wearing him out," I think the key is found in verse 1. It says: "This is the reason you should pray and never give up."

The widow kept pestering the judge in her pursuit of justice and he finally gave in—before she wore him out. I firmly believe that my "prayer warriors" persisted in their requests to God to minimize my pain and to heal me, to the point where they almost wore Him out with their requests! Here I sit in wonderful health, probably at about 95 percent of what I was before this cancer experience. Clearly, God answers prayer!

Each time I reviewed the draft of this writing, reading the e-mails and responses literally put me "back-in-the-moment". I could not get through many of the sections without tears once again welling up in my eyes. I was genuinely blessed by the concern and encouragement shown to Judy and me by so many of my most valiant prayer warriors.

I have maintained loose contact with those physicians who were so integral to the success of my treatment. I would be remiss if I didn't provide an update on them... and also publicly thank them.

Thinking back on Dr. Bonnano, I recall that after I had been in treatment for a little over a week I was looking a little "scruffy" with shaggy hair and needing a shave. Part of the prescription Dr. Bonnano gave me that day was to shave and get a haircut. Being part of the "look sharp, feel sharp, be sharp generation," I understood and complied, mentally thanking him for the nudge.

Dr. Bonnano retired shortly after I completed treatment, but he happened to be in the clinic and working "part time" one afternoon when I accompanied a friend who also had base-of-tongue cancer to the clinic for his radiation treatment. Dr. Bonnano was genuinely glad to see me, as were the technicians that were still there and had put me on that linear accelerator, and lined me up for my treatments those many days. All were glad to see a "success story," which does not happen often enough when dealing with Stage 4 cancer patients.

Dr. Bonnano still practices part-time in Fort Walton Beach.

Dr. Joseph J. Bonnano, MD
Radiation Oncologist
21st Century Radiation Oncology
1026 Mar Walt Drive
Fort Walton Beach, FL
850-863-5294

My Air Force physicians have all separated from the Air Force and are practicing within the civilian community.

As noted previously, Dr. Prieto separated right at the time I was finishing chemotherapy at the Eglin AFB Hospital. It would have been easy for Dr. Prieto to decline taking on that last patient (me) before leaving the Air Force, but he did not and I am much the better because of his professionalism in staying the course right up until the time he separated from the Air Force.

Nor can I overstate the impact of the guidance Dr. Prieto provided regarding optimizing the physical conditions for my success, particularly with the feeding tube. I also appreciated the fact that he did not pull any punches with me regarding the potentially extreme impacts of the chemo and radiation.

Dr. Prieto is in practice in San Angelo, TX.

Robert Prieto, MD
Hematology/Oncology
West Texas Medical Associates
San Angelo, TX 76904
(325)-224-5761

Dr. Prieto was replaced by Dr. Alison Gorrebeeck, who provided my follow-on oncology care for the next two years. Dr. Gorrebeeck established a cancer support group which functioned until she departed Eglin. The group provided valuable insight into dealing with the after effects of the cancer and its treatment. I *strongly* encourage anyone who has dealt with cancer to seek out and participate in a cancer support group.

Dr. Gorrebeeck also educated us on cancer trials for the various forms of cancer being dealt with among the group, drug trials, the drug approval process and advances/changes in potential treatments which might be available and recommended in the event of a cancer recurrence. The information she imparted regarding head-and-neck cancer was especially pertinent to me because we were dealing with a cancer which recurs about 80% of the time within the first two years, 85% within three years, 90 percent within four years and 95% at five years and beyond.

Allison E. Gorrebeeck, MD
Hematology/Oncology
Austin Cancer Center—Lakeway
1401 Medical Parkway
Bldg B, Suite 207
Cedar Park, Texas 78613
(512)-505-5500

Dr. McMurphy separated from the Air Force a year after I completed treatment. I also appreciated that she continued to ask me to mentor some of her head-and-neck cancer patients, which also helped us to maintain contact these last several years.

It is impossible for me to hold a person in higher regard than I do for Dr. McMurphy. Words are not adequate enough for me to express my profound gratitude to Dr. McMurphy. She sets the standard for patient care!

Her current practice is:

Andrea B. McMurphy MD, FACS
Premier Medical
2880 Dauphin St
Mobile, AL 36606
(251)-473-1900.

Dr. Moore picked up my care for the next four years after Dr. McMurphy left the Air Force. During this time, Dr. Moore also recommended to several of his patients that they contact me as a good source of what to expect and how to deal with being treated for a head-and-neck cancer.

Significantly, regarding Dr. Moore, is that Ochsner Health System in New Orleans held a position for him for *more than two years* while he fulfilled his commitment to the Air Force.

Recall that Dr. McMurphy told me that if surgery on the tongue was necessary that Dr. Moore would perform the surgery? I think that was her tacit acknowledgement of Dr. Moore's surgical skills. Those same skills are also why I believe Ochsner was willing to wait such a length of time for Dr. Moore's commitment to the Air Force to end.

I am certain Ochsner made the right choice!

Brian A. Moore, MD, FACS
Chairman
Otorhinolaryngology and Communication Sciences
Director, Head and Neck Surgical Oncology
Ochsner Health System
1514 Jefferson Highway
New Orleans, LA 70121
(504) 842-4080

I offer my highest commendation of these fine physicians to you. You can do no better than them. I also publicly offer them my most profound *"Thank you for taking such good care of me!"*

Even up until now, ten years after completing cancer treatment, I have not made that final call. It is time to do so now.

"Knock It Off!!!"

---

[1] www.cancer.gov/cancertopics/pdq/treatment/oropharyngeal

[2] All e-mails, both those sent and received, maintain their original content. I have elected to include them with only very minor edits for punctuation and spelling in order to maintain the integrity of the writings.

[3] http://www.gelclair.com/

[4] http://www.21stcenturyoncology.com/treat/treat_imrt.html

About the Author

The author is a retired United States Air Force officer who served his country on active duty for more than twenty-nine years--14 years enlisted and 15 years commissioned. After a distinguished career, he continued supporting the Air Force as a contractor for an additional 15 years, finally retiring in 2011.

His Air Force career took him to many unique locations. Among which were South Vietnam, Thailand, the Philippines, South Korea, Saudi Arabia, Alaska, Germany, Spain and England,

He has been married to his wife, Judy, for forty-seven years. They have two children, a daughter and son, both married, with three beautiful and engaging granddaughters.

In spite of wide-ranging travel while in the USAF, they still enjoy traveling, and spending time with family and friends

They live in Niceville, FL., and are actively engaged in their church and community.

As you will note from reading the book, he considers each and every day a genuine blessing!